JOAN

JOAN

The Mysterious Life of the Heretic
Who Became a Saint

DONALD SPOTO

HarperOne
An Imprint of HarperCollinsPublishers

HarperOne

HarperCollins books may be purchased for educational, business, or sales promotional use. For information please write: Special Markets Department, HarperCollins Publishers, 10 East 53rd Street, New York, NY 10022.

HarperCollins Web site: http://www.harpercollins.com
HarperCollins®, ★★®, and HarperOne™ are
trademarks of HarperCollins Publishers.

FIRST HARPERCOLLINS PAPERBACK EDITION PUBLISHED IN 2008

Designed by Joseph Rutt

Library of Congress Cataloging-in-Publication Data is available.
ISBN: 978-0-06-118918-0
ISBN-10: 0-06-118918-9

08 09 10 11 12 RRD(H) 10 9 8 7 6 5 4 3 2 1

for Sue Jett
with love and devotion

Joan: I heard voices telling me what to do. They come from God.
Robert: They come from your imagination.
Joan: Of course. That is how the messages of God come to us.

—George Bernard Shaw,
Saint Joan (1923)

Contents

Foreword

In libraries and on Web sites, you can readily count hundreds of biographies of Joan of Arc published in English since the middle of the nineteenth century. You will find books for the general reader of biography and for the political and social historian; volumes for the religious and military specialist; treatments for children and for adolescents; tracts for those who have preconceived notions about what this teenage girl was or might have been or failed to be or ought to have been; tomes for those who admire and revere her; and works written for those convinced that she was a cunning charlatan, a deluded patriot, a sexually confused peasant limited by a culture of fear and superstition, or a pitiable psychotic.

This vast and diverse collection does not include a thousand books in French and other languages; nor does it take into account novels, poems, songs, hymns, essays, operas, plays, and films with her as the subject. Paintings and statues depicting Joan appear all over the world, and hundreds of churches have been named for her. She is so familiar as to have become, for many people, almost a cliché.

So far as the facts of her life are concerned, it is astonishing to learn that we have more detailed evidence about her than anyone else in the history of the world up to her time. We know far more about Joan, for example, than we do about Moses, Plato, Jesus of Nazareth, Alexander the Great, Julius Caesar, Buddha or Muhammad. For the last two and a half years of her life, we can construct almost a day-by-day account of her whereabouts and actions. We also have several letters she dictated, three of them bearing her simple signature; there is scarcely a single contemporaneous French memoir or chronicle that does not mention Joan the Maid.

Since her death at the age of nineteen in 1431, Joan has fascinated people in many lands. An illiterate girl of remarkable and courageous ingenuity, she boldly confronted a weak and ineffectual heir to the French throne, led rude men in ferocious battles, and was abandoned by the king whose coronation she secured. For all that, her brief presence during the Hundred Years' War turned the tide against rapacious English imperialism and enabled France to survive.

Then, in one of history's most egregious miscarriages of justice, Joan was subjected to a bogus trial on an absurd charge of religious heresy. A rigged jury of churchmen turned her over to the English, and she was burned to death as a heretic. Yet her story does not end there. Joan is unique in that she is the only person to be condemned by a Church court for crimes against religion and faith and then later declared a saint of that same Church, worthy of universal reverence.

IT IS TIME for a new book and a fresh take on this extraordinary young woman. Consider, first of all, the curious nature of the historical record. Recent discoveries are begging for a new look at some key original French and Latin documents in light of modern linguistic studies. I have been researching Joan's life and its sources for over thirty years, collecting documents and trying to keep up with the scholarly work of others, and during this period I have had to revise many of my earlier conclusions.

In the book you are holding, however, I did not wish either to engage in scholarly debate or to invite academic hairsplitting over matters of narrow historical or military interest. Instead, I was gripped by the power and relevance of Joan's life and by her sheer, undiluted faith in the God she believed was guiding her. These are some of the issues that are significant for modern readers.

During Joan's trial hundreds of questions were put to her by the Church court. The interrogations of ecclesiastical judges and theological inquisitors, along with her replies, were recorded each day in French by the chief notary, Guillaume Manchon, and by his two assistants, Guillaume Colles (also called Boisguillaume) and Nicholas Taquel. Every evening the three men compared, collated, and corrected their notes. The original of this document is lost to us, but notarized copies have been preserved at the Bibliothèque Nationale in Paris and the Bibliothèque Municipale in Orléans.

The final and official register of the trial, prepared at the order of the chief judge, Bishop Pierre Cauchon, was based on Manchon's minutes but included much more: in fact, Cauchon ordered the record deliberately falsified at crucial points in order to secure Joan's condemnation and execution. This trial document was completed in Latin by Thomas Courcelles, who was himself one of Joan's judges. He added all the letters from so-called experts as well as Cauchon's instructions and those of Jean Le Maître, the deputy inquisitor for France. Also included were the statements of the faculty of the University of Paris and the opinions of other dignitaries. Five copies of this Latin version were made, and three are extant, all of them signed, notarized, and sealed by Cauchon and Le Maître. They are preserved in Paris at the Bibliothèque de l'Assemblée Nationale and the Bibliothèque Nationale.

The Courcelles manuscript and an enormous cache of authenticated and relevant documents were compiled, edited, and published in five volumes between 1841 and 1849 by French scholar Jules Quicherat, who included documents relative to the second (posthumous) procedure a quarter century after Joan's death—the trial that reversed the condemnation. Unfortunately, Quicherat harmonized several versions

of both long trials and often provided interpretations rather than precise renderings of fifteenth-century French; he also mistranslated many
passages. In 1920 and 1921 Pierre Champion compounded the problems when he brought forth a compact and revised two-volume French
version of Quicherat's work. There have been two English versions of
the trial based on Courcelles/Quicherat: an abridged text, rendered
often roughly, by T. Douglas Murray in 1902, and another by W. P.
Barrett in 1931.

In light of more recent scholarship, Quicherat's edition was edited
and newly translated into French from 1960 to 1971 by Pierre Tisset
and Yvonne Lanhers, whose scholarship included reference to a crucial document at the Bibliothèque Municipale d'Orléans. Its author
and precise date are unknown, but its final form probably comes to
us from about 1500, and it provides Joan's actual words at the trial.
This manuscript (known simply as the "Orléans" text) essentially
replaces the trial as replicated by Quicherat and is indispensable for
modern study; I cite it here with my own translations. W. S. Scott's
abridged and reconstructed version (1956) was the first in English to
use the Orléans manuscript, and to it almost all of my predecessors
have turned. But the edition of Tisset and Lanhers deserved far more
careful study.

AT THIS POINT serious problems emerge that I tried to remedy in
this book. Little recently published material on Joan has taken into
account the magisterial work of Pierre Duparc, who from 1977 to 1989
published in five volumes the original Latin and French testimonies and
all documentation relevant to the nullification trial of 1455–1456, cast-
ing a bright light on the life of Joan before her brief military career and
her early death. Only very short passages based on Duparc's scholarship have so far appeared in English, and those selections are poorly
edited and badly translated. I redress this imbalance at least in part by

presenting my own translations of representative sections of these documents. These greatly expand our understanding of Joan's life, mission, purpose and convictions. I was guided, of course, by the work of scholars who preceded me, not only in studying the trials but also in considering the accounts of Joan written during and immediately after her lifetime. I am grateful most of all to the International Joan of Arc Society, a group whose resources are noted at the beginning of my bibliography.

BY 2004 I was more than ever convinced that, in addition to providing an unbiased consideration of up-to-the-minute textual evidence, a fresh look at this extraordinary life might show the profound significance of Joan of Arc for our own time. We live in a twenty-first-century climate of international fear and suspicion, and to us this fifteenth-century European girl has something startling and important to say.

Joan fought and died to preserve the identity and particularity of a sovereign place; she dedicated herself to the unique and irreplaceable soul of a country. She did not believe that it was right for her country to be—as it had already become in part and was dangerously close to becoming completely—simply a fiefdom of the kingdom of England.

To use modern terms, she was horrified at the thought that the integrity of her country should be sacrificed to foreign empire-building. Whatever France was not yet and whatever it needed to be, she dedicated herself to its enduring existence. Joan was an unwitting architect of the idea that every nation is inviolable—that no people may be overrun, dominated, suppressed or brought to the brink of annihilation by an outside force. She stands for the injunction, later ratified by declarations, treaties and covenants signed all over the civilized world, that no nation (without direct provocation and an immediate threat to its survival) may invade, much less annihilate, another country in order to turn it into a cog in the machine of mightier people eager for economic exploitation and territorial expansion. In this regard, Joan speaks clearly to the political life of the twenty-first century.

BUT WHAT ABOUT the visions she claimed to see and the voices she heard, all of which she said were "from God"? Despite the problems in her telling and the apparent contradictions that becloud her statements, I believe that her spiritual experiences were profoundly valid and that they convey something of the truth. This assertion needs to be tested and challenged, however, without assuming either that her "visions" and "voices" are to be taken at literal face value or to be discounted because such phenomena do not or cannot "really" occur. The latter is little more than circular reasoning: such and such cannot happen because it does not happen. More helpful is to ask, "How do we assess the claims that it has indeed happened?"

Those who regard Joan as a saint usually assume both her veracity and the "facts" of the visions and voices. But I believe it is critical to ask what such visions and voices meant in fifteenth-century France. What did they mean to Joan, and how was she forced to adapt her speech to describe spiritual experiences that transcend ordinary language? Can some sort of validity be granted to them—however we understand them—in light of a consistent pattern of character and action in her life? This is a matter neglected by other biographers of Joan; it is a major theme of this book.

In this regard it is important to consider the nature of religious language in general, which is always inadequate, symbolic and metaphorical, never fully communicating spiritual experience. As I have tried to demonstrate, Joan's "problem," like that of religious visionaries throughout history, was to report an ineffable experience, to find some sort of expression within the currency of her own religious and cultural forms. Like the great Hebrew visionary prophets of antiquity, the mystics of every faith, and the great poets and lovers of history, Joan struggled with the inadequacy of human speech to express what cannot be fully expressed but that somehow must be expressed.

What about, also, her vowed virginity as a laywoman, which to some modern minds at once suggests a mental aberration or at least sexual dysfunction? We might ask, rather, what did virginity mean to European people six centuries ago? What did it mean for this girl? Answers to these questions should not be prejudicially or casually given.

Only by interpreting Joan's life in light of her times and her language constructs can we begin to understand her. She was not a seventeenth-century Italian girl, a nineteenth-century English maiden, or a twentieth-century American teenager. The specifics of her time, place, language, religion and economy must be carefully considered if we are to gain something close to a realistic picture of her rather than one that merely reflects our own bias or fantasy or our own (also limited) twenty-first-century experience. Only by interpreting her words and gestures in light of her own time and place—only by giving them context and trying to understand what they meant for her and her contemporaries—can we come close to her. We are looking for a girl who lived in an era and a place vastly different from our own—she is Joan of Arc, not Joan of Arkansas.

Interpretation is a word that alienates many people, as if it means falsifying, fabricating or exaggerating. But to understand, it is essential to interpret. Interpreters are those who try to find the threads of meaning woven through history and in lives—to reveal why certain happenings became events and why certain people of long ago did not vanish into obscurity.

JOAN WAS NOT sophisticated in matters of religion or religious language, nor did she follow a program designed by the Church in general or by a religious community in particular. Her way was not one of pious practices but one of absolute trust, of unwavering faith that God would not abandon her or the people of France. However we interpret her voices and visions, it is clear that to her spiritual sight, this world is not the sum of reality. For Joan, the realm of matter and the world of the spirit were not two hermetically sealed dimensions of reality but rather one continuum: the earth was completely interpenetrated with the things of God. Hence she knew—by intuition, not by learning—the necessary congruence of justice with love.

Neither wife nor nun, neither queen nor noblewoman, neither philosopher nor stateswoman, Joan of Arc represents something that was fresh then and is still pertinent now for anyone, and perhaps most poignantly for women. In the final analysis, her battle was not with English politicians but with the powerful of the Church. Dedicated to her faith, she was betrayed by its earthly institution; abandoned by everyone for whom she fought, she was blithely handed over to a death that was illegally maneuvered and hideously exacted. In her terror, her loneliness, and her agony she remains a figure of starkest simplicity.

This book deals with what might be called the mystery of Joan of Arc, and I offer it within the belief that the world and everything in it belongs to God and matters to God. A mystery is not a puzzle, a problem, or something to be worked out or resolved, and Joan is not an intellectual challenge. In the vocabulary of theology, a mystery is an event, action or person pointing to the presence of the hidden but real God, who enters time and space.

In this regard, and in her passionate insistence unto death that an individual nation matters within the great chain of being, Joan of Arc may be a powerful contemporary sign of the transforming power of faith.

ONE

Of War and Occupation

(1412–1423)

The tiny village of Domrémy, in eastern France, seems hardly to have changed in the last six centuries. At the beginning of the fifteenth century it held fewer than two hundred people living in small houses, from which they went out to work as farmers and vintners. Although on the frontier of the duchy of Lorraine, Domrémy was ruled by and loyal to the kingdom of France. Perched on the left bank of the River Meuse, the village had been mostly spared the ravages of the Black Death, but not its widespread economic effects or the depredations of mercenaries on both sides of the Hundred Years' War, that series of skirmishes great and small between England and France. When the royal purse or residual idealism was lacking to encourage soldiers, men outfitted with little more than bow and arrow simply roamed through the countryside, pillaging, raping, purloining livestock and generally terrorizing the locals, who otherwise peacefully herded their flocks and tilled the soil.

The medieval tradition of serfdom had mostly disappeared; instead of owing their labors and lives to a vassal or lord, French peasants in places like the Meuse Valley could become as affluent as aristocrats: they had property to which they paid cash rent to a local *seigneur*, but they enjoyed the benefits of ownership and could increase their land-holdings.

In 1400 Jacques d'Arc was an enterprising, respected landowner in Domrémy; by 1423 he was also the local *doyen*, bearing both the honor and responsibility of collecting village taxes and supervising the defense of citizens and livestock in times of assault. He was born about 1375 in Ceffonds, twenty miles west of Domrémy, but some historians theorize that his parents must have lived in Arc-en-Barrois, farther south. Their argument is based on the assumption that this location explains *d'Arc*, indicating the place from which Jacques came—a *nom d'origine*, often given to notable or honored citizens. But if Jacques had indeed hailed from Arc-en-Barrois, the local Latin manuscripts (the first to mention the family) would have identified him as "Jacques de Arco," in the con-temporary style of patronymics. Further complicating matters is the fact that before the invention of printing in 1440 spelling was not stan-dardized, and so the family name appears variously as Darc, Dars, Day, Darx, Dare, Tarc, Tart or Dart.

After living in Domrémy several years, Jacques had what might be called middle-class status. He owned about fifty acres of farmland and pasture on the edge of the village as well as cattle, sheep and a furnished home. The house was typical, with a slate roof resting on wooden beams, a hard-packed dirt floor inside, and a few rooms, some of them with a small window; year-round, the place tended to be damp and fetid. A single fireplace, in the main room just inside the front door, was used for warmth and cooking; here too the family dined and the parents slept. Water had to be hauled up from the river, and of course there was noth-ing like a bathroom: instead, people found all kinds of uses for the back-yard. A wooden staircase led to an attic used for storing grain. At that time the d'Arc house would have been considered almost luxurious.*

---

* Alterations have not destroyed the original layout of the house of Jacques d'Arc, which may be visited to this day. The village is now known as Domrémy-la-Pucelle, thus honoring its celebrated daughter.

The small home was sufficient to accommodate a few pilgrims (without fee) or merchants (for a modest fee) who stopped in the village on their way to more prestigious towns. According to witnesses, visitors were treated with legendary kindness and warmth by Jacques's wife, Isabelle Romée, who had come from Vouthon, four miles from Domrémy; her second name was commonly conferred on those who had completed a religious pilgrimage to Rome. For centuries, such a pious journey had indicated profound devotion: traveling to sacred sites—to Rome, for example, where the apostles Peter and Paul were believed to have been martyred—was difficult, expensive and unsafe in any season. Women, even in the company of clergy, were easy targets of brigands, rapists and highwaymen.

At home, Isabelle's primary task was to raise her children as good Christians and to see that they knew their prayers. She and Jacques had three boys and two girls: Jacques or Jacquemin; Jehan or Jean; Pierre or Pierrelot; Jehanne or Jeanne; and Catherine. Jean and Pierre appear later in the story; of Jacques and Catherine almost nothing is known except that the latter married at about the age of sixteen and died soon after.

The name Jehanne is rooted in the late Latin Johanna, the feminine of Johannes, or John; in English the name takes many forms, among them Joan, Jean, Joanne or Jane. Jehanne was often (and eventually always) written as Jeanne, which was how the name was and is pronounced (the *h* being silent). "In my country," she said, referring to her region, "people called me Jeannette [the affectionate diminutive for Jeanne], but they called me Jeanne when I came into France," which meant, at the time, the central part of the kingdom, where the royal court could be found and the monarch resided.

As for her established name in history, chroniclers and poets of her time (and she herself) never referred to "Joan of Arc." The appellation "Johanna Darc" was first used twenty-five years after her death, at the trial striking down the validity of the court that sentenced and condemned her. The first accounts in English simply translated what was considered to be her father's *nom d'origine*, and so she was identified as Joan of Arc. The use of surnames was unusual at the time, but had she assumed or been given one, it would very likely have been, as was the custom, her mother's, Romée. For her part, things were much simpler: Joan referred to herself as simply "the Maid."

IT HAS BEEN customary to fix Joan's birth in 1411 or 1412. Not long before her death in 1431 she was asked her age: "Nineteen or thereabouts," she replied, which was a customary formula: Latin court records during the Middle Ages noted a person's age as *vel circiter, vel circa, vel eocirca*—"thereabouts." People had no care for their precise age, nor did they make any effort to establish it. Our modern concern for specifics such as date, place of birth, and legal status was unknown to medieval society. In Joan's time, as one scholar has noted, "Historiographers and chroniclers were just beginning to record the birth dates of kings and very great noblemen; at the same period, parish registers were beginning to be kept here and there," but this was rare, and most church registers did not start recording data until the late sixteenth century.

As for the month and day of her birth, that was later put at January 6, for symbolic reasons. The Western Christian liturgical calendar marks the Feast of the Epiphany on that date, the revelation to the world of the heavenly kingship of Jesus Christ. It was natural for Joan's partisans to indicate a parallel between that religious feast and her birth, for it was she who eventually arranged for the formal anointing of Charles VII as earthly king.

Until she was twelve or thirteen, there was nothing remarkable about Joan's life. Those who knew her and her family gave sworn testimony years later as to basic facts. Joan's parents, according to a neighboring farmer named Jean Moreau, were "faithful Catholics and hard workers with a good reputation." As Joan herself told her interrogators, so Moreau testified: she was baptized by the local priest, Jean Minet, in the parish church of Saint-Rémy, for whom Domrémy was named. The name Jeanne honored two of her godmothers and five godfathers named Jean.

The title of godmother or godfather, as today, was honorific and indicated a witness to baptism rather than a spiritual teacher; Joan always insisted that her mother was her sole source of religious instruction. On the first day of her trial, Joan said quite plainly that she had learned only from her mother the words of the Lord's Prayer, the Ave Maria and the Credo. "From childhood," Moreau added, "she was raised in the faith and imbued with good morals."

Like almost everyone at the time—except for men with clerical, university or court jobs in sight—Joan was not taught to read or write, and only later could she sign her name to a document. Apart from what she heard in parish sermons, she had no schooling except from her mother, who taught her the domestic arts of spinning and sewing, at which she became quite adept; as Joan told her accusers in 1431, she did not think any woman in Rouen could teach her anything about these crafts. She also helped her father and her siblings take the livestock out to pasture. As for religious education, she would have learned about the sacraments from the village priest, and she knew Bible episodes through sermons at Mass. Regular and frequent churchgoing also provided a kind of religious education through paintings, statues and church windows, whose images told of events in the life of Christ and the saints.

"Sometimes she went off to church when her parents thought she was in the fields," Moreau continued, "and she went to Mass quite often." In her religious exercises she was both exact and faithful, and her piety was marked by a willing spontaneity. As a neighbor called Béatrice Estellin remembered, there were no airs or attitudes in her conduct, nothing of compulsion or trepidation, nothing merely dutiful.

Girlhood friends like Hauviette and Mengette remembered Joan as "good and sweet.... She went devotedly to church, but she kept herself busy, did the housework, and watched over her father's flocks." A local plowman named Simonin Musnier had endured a number of childhood illnesses; as he recalled, "When I was sick, Joan came to comfort me." Isabellette d'Epinal added that Joan "willingly gave money to the poor and welcomed them [to the family house]. She preferred to sleep under the mantel so that the poor could have her bed."

As for this evident piety, it was not so rare at a time when faith and its practice were mainstream aspects of medieval life; indeed, to be a European meant to be a citizen of both the temporal and spiritual realms comprising Christendom. The intellectual notions of agnosticism or atheism did not exist; it was universally accepted that the world belonged to God and was permeated with His presence. Hence the language of faith was like a common country in which all people lived, and this gave them a certain stability and social cohesion, whatever the state of the region or the institutional Church. Joan was diligent regarding prayer and worship, but she had no connection to monasteries or convents, and apparently she never considered becoming a nun.

Until she was about thirteen, there was very little to distinguish her from her peers or her siblings. She was raised, as the saying went, between home and the fields: she spun and sewed; she helped with household tasks; she took her turn guarding her father's flocks and assisted with gardening. She played games with her friends, and she sang and danced in the fields and around festival trees, frequently decorated for religious feasts.

BUT LIFE WAS not usually predictable or secure. The open hostilities of the Hundred Years' War between England and France defined life for everyone. The tensions and clashes, the battles and quarrels, the negotiations, truces and betrayals had always simmered and once again roiled violently and more widely when Joan was a child. There was also civil war, for France was not yet a unified nation but rather a shifting political entity composed of a number of small realms, duchies, counties and petty states.

At the core of the Hundred Years' War lay a long conflict over the relationship between the closely related dynasties of England and France; also at stake was the uncertain rapport between France and its essentially independent feudal princes, the powerful dukes of Aquitaine and Burgundy. Inconveniently, the Duke of Aquitaine was also the king of England, while the Duke of Burgundy controlled that region as well as Flanders, portions of the Low Countries, and areas along the German border.

The war began over the matter of succession to the French throne. In 1328 Charles IV of France, last of the three sons of Philip IV, died without a male heir. The crown was then claimed by two cousins: Philip of Valois, Philip IV's nephew; and by King Edward III of England, Philip IV's grandson by his daughter. But the Valois court invoked the Salic law, which banned royal birthright through the female line. Legal as well as military courts on both sides accumulated arguments in favor of Philip or Edward, but a French high court decided in favor of the Valois line and rejected the claims of the Plantagenet dynasty.

For King Edward, France was not merely a symbolic hereditary ornament for England; it was the wealthiest and most heavily populated country in Christendom. His goal was, therefore, to make the English monarch ruler of both France and England, thereby expanding and confirming bonds that had existed since the Battle of Hastings and continued through Henry II's marriage to Eleanor of Aquitaine, which for a time had brought most of southwest France under English rule. And so, as the new Valois dynasty surely expected, Edward did not abandon his imperial aspirations. In 1337 he sent troops to engage Philip, now King Philip VI, in outright combat. Nothing less than the future of a country was at stake.

For the next twenty-five years, the English were consistently victorious in episodic battles, annexing more and more French territories.
Charles V of France recovered much of the land gained by England, but
this advantage was subsequently lost after his death in 1380, when feudal rivalries erupted between factions loyal to the Duke of Burgundy
(aligned with England) and the Duke of Orléans (loyal to France).

WHEN JOAN WAS a child, her king was the unfortunate Charles VI;
aptly called Charles the Mad, he was occasionally lucid but was mostly
a lunatic. With the literal and legal breakdown of the French court and
the demoralization of French troops, it was comparatively easy for the
English to win complete victories in 1415 and 1417, when Joan was
still a child. Their successes gave the Anglo-Burgundian alliance control of the Aquitaine and all France north of the Loire except for a few
loyalist towns, and Paris fell to the English in 1419. Thus Henry V of
England became the single most powerful political and diplomatic
authority in Europe.

When Jean, Duke of Burgundy, was assassinated in 1419 the partisans of Charles VI and his son, the dauphin or rightful heir, were
blamed for the murder. For this reason Jean's son Philip, the new Duke
of Burgundy, no longer supported the Valois and gave his allegiance to
England. He and those on his side were known as Burgundians, while
those loyal to the crown of France were known as the Armagnac party,
which took its name from Bernard, count of Armagnac.

That same year Burgundians ravaged Armagnac strongholds and
even the modest homes of ordinary pro-Valois citizens. Anticipating
possible skirmishes and worse near Domrémy, Joan's father and another farmer pooled their resources in order to use the Château de l'Île, a
modest fort on an island in the Meuse, where they planned to house
local families and livestock in the event of pitched battle in the village.

In 1420 Philip of Burgundy threw his support behind the Treaty of

Troyes, which gave Charles VI's daughter to Henry of England to be his wife; the treaty further stipulated that their heir would be king of the single but twofold realm of England and France. This contract effectively annulled the right of Charles's surviving son—the dauphin, or direct heir to the throne, also called Charles. Among those Burgundians who helped negotiate the treaty to the benefit of the English was a clergyman named Pierre Cauchon, who was rewarded with the bishopric of Beauvais.

Both Henry V and Charles VI died within weeks of one another in 1422, but the war was zealously prosecuted on the English side by Henry's brother, John of Lancaster, the Duke of Bedford, who was regent for Henry's son, the infant King Henry VI. Cauchon, all the while, labored on behalf of the English government in France, which was headquartered in Rouen, northwest of Paris in Normandy.

The dauphin was now nominally King Charles VII, but he was uncrowned, and in this state of royal limbo he remained for seven years, in residence at the large castle of Chinon, one hundred fifty miles southwest of Paris. Being uncrowned was not a mere technicality: as long as Charles VII did not travel north to the cathedral of Reims (where French kings had been anointed since 1179), his claim of kingship could be—and was—much contested. At the same time, English forces gained astonishing strength and were prepared to deal once and for all with the dauphin, whose war chest was virtually depleted and whose officers and soldiers were exhausted and ill trained. By 1425 French military discipline was all but nonexistent, and the troops themselves were rapacious and unprincipled: the situation had reached critical mass.

Given these conditions, the Duke of Bedford made elaborate plans for a blockade and occupation at Orléans, a vital commercial town sixty miles south of Paris; that strategy would provide him with access to the dauphin's refuge at Chinon. As this news spread, the complete collapse of France seemed imminent.

• • •

DOMRÉMY, UNDER THE jurisdiction of the military governor at nearby Vaucouleurs, supported the Valois dynasty of France and was thus staunchly Armagnac, but just across the Meuse—little more than a brook in the countryside—lay the village of Maxey, ardently Burgundian. The larger engagements of the war often had their complement in the petty fights and rivalries of children who were neighbors.

As to Joan's knowledge of the political and military situation, nothing can be said with certainty. She may have learned something from conversations between her parents and among villagers, but what detail was available is impossible to know. The main issue, however, was clear to everyone: there had been a long and bitter struggle to determine if the English and their Burgundian allies would set the crown of France on the offspring of Henry V, or if the partisans of the Valois would emerge triumphant and France would survive. Just when international consciousness was being seeded all over Europe, the existence of France itself was threatened. Precisely at this time, the ordinariness of Joan's life was forever altered.

TWO

Visions

(1424–1427)

By 1424 conditions favorable to the French cause were rapidly deteriorating, as were the prestige and influence of the Roman Church. To this day people sometimes express astonishment that the pope did not intervene in the conflict between England and France or that bishops were not dispatched to sue for peace or that there seemed to be no Church voices speaking against the threat to the very existence of a people. But the moral authority of Rome itself had been seriously compromised by a lust for power and by frank corruption. At such times, remarkable women often arose whose influence benefited both Church and state; Joan would become but one in a tradition of counselors.

During the spring of 1378 Bartolomeo Prignano was elected to the papacy, which he assumed under the name Urban VI. As early as that summer, his previous competence as an administrator was diminished by unmistakable signs of a sinister side to his personality: Pope Urban became so mentally unstable and publicly abusive, even toward those prelates who had elected him, that a number of the French cardinals urged him to abdicate. Without waiting for his reply, they put out the word that Urban had been deposed; later he went so far as to arrange for five of these critics to be tortured and executed.

In October of the same year, the French elected a replacement pope, who took office as Clement VII; Urban, however, remained at his post. So began the Great Western Schism, a forty-year period when at least two men and sometimes three claimed to be pope, each alternately excommunicating the other and accepting money and arms from different European countries in support of their causes. The ecclesiastical chaos was monumental, the demoralization of ordinary Christians pervasive.

Before he completely lost control of himself, Urban VI found his papacy defended by none other than Catherine of Siena, a profoundly mystical character who experienced intense religious visions and turned from an early life of reclusive contemplation to become a vigorous worker for Church unity and reform, nursing the sick and dying during the plague of 1374. She was linked to the Dominican Order as a tertiary, a laywoman living not in a convent but rather in the world, usually at home. Her good works consisted mostly of charitable service to the poor, and her ideals and prayers were inspired by the religious life of Dominican friars.

But Catherine became intensely involved in politics. She wielded, for example, enormous influence on the clergy in northern Italy as well as on the pope in self-imposed Avignon exile. She feared neither prince nor cleric: of the disgraceful conduct of too many clergymen, for example, she wrote candidly, "Bloated with pride, they devour money meant for the poor and spend it on their own pleasures!" At Urban's personal invitation, she traveled to Rome within days of his election to help shore up support for his cause. But when Catherine was threatened and very nearly assassinated by Urban's enemies, he sent her no guard and consistently ignored the danger to which she was then exposed on his behalf. Worn out from her habit of extreme penances and a lifetime of excessive fasting and travels, she died in 1380, still in her thirties. Catherine of Siena was canonized in 1461.

The Council of Constance deposed two claimants to the papacy, forced a third to abdicate, and in 1417 installed as pope a layman

named Oddo Colonna. He had to be hastily ordained priest and consecrated bishop, after which he took office as Pope Martin V, thus effectively ending the schism. Almost alone among premodern popes,
Martin is remembered as a sympathetic friend to the disenfranchised
Jews of Europe. He condemned anti-Semitism and strictly forbade the
forced baptism of Jewish children, which unfortunately had been prac-
ticed in medieval Italy.

During his papacy Martin was preoccupied with the politics of the
Roman situation and, lacking reliable or timely reports, had little
access to news of conditions elsewhere, especially since the French
bishops faced their own internal dilemmas and had to decide whether
they were Burgundian or Armagnac; most of them now solidly backed
the victorious English. Living in the spirit of Jesus of Nazareth seemed
a forgotten ideal for many clergymen, obsessed as they were with
shoring up their own wealth against the encroachments of secular
princes. In fact, it was often left to devout women like Catherine of
Siena to issue calls to reform: she went so far as to reprimand Urban
to his face.

Earlier, the German abbess Hildegard of Bingen in the twelfth century had also exerted influence far beyond the walls of her nunnery. She
wrote letters to Henry II of England, urging him to avoid the company
of those who would kill his friend Thomas Becket; alas, her injunction
was ignored. She also wrote to Henry's wife, Eleanor of Aquitaine,
comforting her during the times of her husband's infidelities. In Italy,
Angela of Foligno was a spiritual counselor to communities of disaf-
fected Franciscan friars, and Birgitta of Sweden was not afraid to scold
churchmen and bishops openly on account of their negligence and
moral laxity. From the time of the early Church, history in every era
bears the names of countless women who often accomplished what
men could not or would not dare.

* * *

AT ABOUT NOON one summer day in 1424, when she was in her father's garden, Joan sensed that she was surrounded by a great light. She also heard, as she said later, "a revelation from God by a voice," which told her to be devout, to pray, to frequent the sacraments, and always to rely on the Lord for help. Although at first very much frightened by the light and the voice (who wouldn't be?), she was soon consoled by them, and these experiences continued—precisely how often and at what times, she never specified. Nor, for the time being, did she identify the voice or voices; they were simply "of God" or "from God." In addition, she told no one of these extraordinary experiences.

The third time this happened, Joan knew that she heard the "voice of an angel," as she put it; in other words, what the voice told her was appropriate to the counsel of the angels, of the heavenly court itself. Over the next three years she was summoned by the voices "to come to the aid of the king of France"; eventually she was also told just how to accomplish that. At first Joan protested that she was only a poor girl who could neither ride a warhorse nor lead men in battle. But she could not for long ignore the directions, and she placed her honor and her faith in God, Who, she was assured, would supply what she lacked.

The voices and the light continued to come to Joan throughout 1425, when Domrémy was raided by Burgundians. However irregularly, these spiritual experiences endured as long as she lived. But until she was on trial, in 1431, she spoke of her experiences only to two confidants, never to her parents or to her parish priest. Part of the reason for her silence must have been fear of rejection, and part was surely the difficulty in putting an ineffable experience into words.

To "see" the angels and the light and to "hear" the voices referred to a kind of sight and hearing that do not necessarily come through the physical senses. Her perception was not intuitive daydreaming or a psychological conviction about something. What mattered for Joan was not the physical sight of spiritual beings or saints, much less a retelling or an embellished account of the sight by her or anyone else. What mattered was that the message came, as she believed, from God. The important thing, in short, was not what she saw or how she saw it, but the inner revelation, the compelling sense that she was purposefully addressed.

Although it happened to Joan on a far more profound (not to say more dramatic) level, the situation was rather like that of someone who "hears" a call when seeing something in art or reading about it in a book: a summons is felt—to a career, perhaps, or to a new commitment. One "sees" and recalls the familiar work of art or the episode in a book but in a new and deeper way and more emphatically, as it is now connected to a sense of personal destiny or purpose. But this is only an analogy of the mystic experience that touched Joan.

Ultimately, she said that God had guided her by means of heavenly visitations from Saint Michael the Archangel, Saint Catherine of Alexandria, and Saint Margaret of Antioch; later she also mentioned that she had seen Gabriel the archangel and a large company of angels. It is critical to recall that the transcripts of her trial are the only source for our knowledge of Joan's spiritual experience, and it is clear from the texts that her answers to the judges' questions were ambiguous and often contradictory. But one thing is clear: Joan claimed to hear voices and see visions, and always there was light—"a great deal of light on all sides," she said. Once she was a prisoner, from 1430, the light was focused on Catherine and Margaret, and she described them as she did Michael—sometimes precisely, at other times hazily.

Reading the trial documents, we sense her frustration in trying to articulate what cannot be fully articulated: "I do not recognize them at once." Day after day Joan was forced to repeat statements, often out of context, and to add details that were irrelevant or frankly absurd, such as the color of her heavenly visitors' hair and clothing. Under interrogation by a swarm of judges trying daily to trap her, and exhausted by battles, she was kept in appalling prison cells, denied adequate food, and threatened and humiliated each day; it is not surprising that her responses became confused and often indistinct. But her mystical experiences gave her sufficient confidence that, as the trial notes put it on March 3, "she said she would do better to obey her sovereign Lord God rather than men."

PRECISELY BECAUSE OF her visions, Joan of Arc becomes for very many people an intolerable conundrum, almost or entirely someone who cannot be taken seriously. At the same time, any assessment of the last six years of her life depends to a great extent on her credibility, her maturity, and indeed her sanity. And so summary judgments are often made, based on how one judges her "voices" or how one understands her political significance for France or her place in the religious history of the world.

Most problematic for the skeptics is the matter of the angels and archangels Joan claimed to have seen and heard.

Angels were part of ancient, pre-Semitic iconography, and their images were taken over and presumed in Hebrew, Christian and Islamic theology from the earliest times to the present. Initially, before Hebrew faith was monotheistic, angels resembled their Babylonian and Assyrian counterparts: minor deities or part of a heavenly court. For the Hebrews, "an angel of the Lord" was a way both of avoiding direct mention of the divine name and of indicating divine activity in the affairs of the world; angels occur in the Jewish Scriptures as guides, consolers, and monitors. When they are described as quite distinct beings, not all angels were regarded as good or benevolent, as the book of Job and the Jewish apocryphal literature attest.

Angels were mostly described as attendants in the realm of God, and, because it would have been blasphemous in Judaism to imply the direct apprehension of God by mortals, angels were often depicted as legates or messengers, bearers of inspiration and of divine commands.

Indeed, the word *angel* comes from the Greek *angelos*, which translates the Hebrew *mal'ak;* both words mean "messenger."

Similarly, the annunciation scenes in the New Testament infancy narratives of Matthew and Luke emphasize not these curious beings (who are never described), but rather the astonishing, unbidden divine initiative in bringing John the Baptist and Jesus of Nazareth into the world. After that, angels are only infrequently mentioned in the Christian Scriptures—at the desert temptation of Jesus, at the agony in Gethsemane, and at the discovery of the Resurrection. They are remarkably absent during his ministry.

Since biblical times the existence of angels as individual spiritual beings has been taken for granted by many people. But however we understand them, it is important to emphasize that angels represent something much more than grotesque, fantastic winged figures and something more powerful than could be conveyed by philosophic discourse. Ancient Greeks had a talent for abstraction and conceptualizing, but Hebrew thought was notable for its particularity. In this regard, angels dramatically represent God's presence and actions among His people.*

In the Hebrew Scriptures the archangel Michael is mentioned only in the book of Daniel (second century B.C.), where he appears as both a guardian spirit and a personification of the people. In the New Testament his name occurs twice: the letter of Jude points to an obscure reference to Michael in the Assumption of Moses, an apocryphal Jewish work; and the book of Revelation refers to "Michael and his angels battling against the dragon [of sin]." In medieval France Michael the Archangel was the special patron of soldiers fighting against faithless armies: he was always invoked with prayerful songs amid battles. The flags of the dauphin himself were painted with Michael's image: to fight

---

* A widespread obsession with angels in the late twentieth and early twenty-first centuries may be a sign of a certain decadence of religion. In popular entertainments angels are presented as kindly policemen, wise aunts or down-home psychologists. They are not much different from friendly aliens, but they dress better.

for the heir to the throne meant to fight on the side of the heavenly choirs.

Michael had been for centuries the patron of the French royal family, and the coastal stronghold of Mont-Saint-Michel represented France's ancient Christian roots; its abbey and fortress remained loyal to the dauphin. The French locations named for him are too numerous to list: one has only to think of the Boulevard Saint-Michel in Paris and the colossal baroque statue (a few steps from the Seine, at the Place Saint-Michel) depicting Michael with a sword, vanquishing the dragon of sin—an image drawn from Revelation. Up to the end of the nineteenth century, France kept Saint Michael's Day (September 29) as a great religious feast and holiday. Such a heroic spiritual figure was known to Joan from childhood, when she lived in the duchy of Bar, whose patron saint was Michael; at least forty-six churches in neighboring dioceses were dedicated to him.

DEVOTION TO CATHERINE of Alexandria was widespread in medieval Europe, although she was not mentioned anywhere before the ninth century. During the violent persecution of Christians under the Roman emperor Maximinus from 235 to 238, so the legend went, eighteen-year-old Catherine approached the tyrant, condemned his cruelty, and confounded his belief in Roman polytheism by her impressive intellectual discourse. Unable to contradict her logical arguments, Maximinus had her tortured and imprisoned. Catherine, however, was not to be stopped: even in chains she succeeded in converting jailers, other prisoners, and even the emperor's wife, who came to visit her. Livid with rage, the emperor had Catherine beheaded after more dreadful tortures.

As told for six centuries, this was a dramatic and edifying story, but it turned out to be wildly fictitious, and in 1969 Catherine of Alexandria was quietly removed from the Catholic Church's official roll of saints (along with others, such as Christopher and Barbara). The existence of early martyrs is well documented in secular and sacred writings, and the story of Catherine represents a type of heroic Christian during the first three centuries after Jesus; indeed, she stands for countless anonymous believers who died for their faith. But as told, the story is apocryphal.

The legend of Catherine was, however, dear to the hearts of medieval Christians, who found their own religious truth in accounts of her life and death. Many chapels were dedicated to Catherine in Europe, and statues of her were found throughout France. Joan's sister was named Catherine, and a church dedicated to the saint sat in nearby Maxey. On Saint Catherine's feast day each year, work was prohibited and families gathered for worship.

Set before the devout as a model of Christian heroism, Catherine was also the subject of many French sermons and poems. She was the primary patroness of young girls and of students who had to debate learned colleagues and professors; in other words, Catherine was just the sort of heroine Joan herself would have taken for model and intercessor, a saint whose name and reputation had been close to her since childhood and to whom she would naturally turn during the harrowing year of her imprisonment and interrogation—the circumstances when she first identified Catherine's among the voices she heard.

Margaret of Antioch was equally popular at the time, singled out for special devotion in the region where Joan was born and raised. Like Catherine of Alexandria, Margaret was supposed to have lived at the time of the early Christian persecutions. When she converted to Christianity and consecrated her virginity to God, she was disowned by her pagan father. A Roman prefect then saw the beautiful teenage Margaret tending sheep and tried to seduce her. When she refused him, he publicly denounced her as a Christian, and after numerous tortures she too was beheaded. She became the special patroness of falsely accused people, and her statue had a prominent place in Joan's parish church. Margaret was precisely the kind of young, courageous virgin whose fidelity unto death would have comforted Joan during her interrogations.

Michael, Catherine and Margaret: widely venerated, they were especially close figures in the minds of ordinary Christians in medieval France. Joan knew about them; she saw them represented in paintings, stained-glass windows, and statues; and she would have prayed to them in her crises. Some modern scholars dismiss the possibility of a transcendent revelation to Joan with this explanation: forced to identify the voices during her trial, they say, she would naturally have mentioned those whose stories and images were familiar.

But simply because she mentioned these saints late, when she was compelled to identify the voices, it does not follow that those identities occurred to her only on the spot. Indeed, she had been keeping a deep silence about them for a number of good reasons. And despite the fact that the "voices" seem to be from those whose very existence is dubious, the *experience* mediated to Joan by these voices was never in doubt, at least to her.

FROM THE HEBREW prophet Isaiah to the present, each era finds its own terms to describe what is unknowable, opaque, or mysterious. Once upon a time we described the mentally ill as possessed by demons. Later they were considered victims of disordered humors. In both cases they were ostracized, chained in dungeons, submitted to various tortures, regarded as sinners, and simply allowed to expire. Now we often say that such a person is, for example, a paranoid schizophrenic with an Oedipus complex, or we study his genetic history and seek to learn the chemical or genealogical sources for the disorder.

But scientific labels do not enable us to understand the etiology or substance of madness any more than did "demonic possession." How is it that one can suffer a loss of personality and reason? Even as we

attach comforting terms that give us a way of dealing with the awfulness of the plight, we know that scientific and psychological jargon
simply enables us to have a coping mechanism and, we hope, to deal
more compassionately with sufferers.

In Joan's case it is tempting to take refuge in psychiatric terminol-
ogy, thus reducing her marvelous experiences to meaninglessness.
Some have argued that Joan had an inner ear infection producing
sounds resembling whispering voices or that an eye affliction could
have made bright sunlight intolerable and given her the idea that she
was seeing the outlines of forms. But this explanation runs afoul of the
fact that she rode horses, was upright in battle, and made stunning
logistic decisions in broad daylight. Still others are convinced that the
girl was a victim of benign autosuggestion, of hallucinations and delusions of grandeur. But Joan's consequent actions reveal a wholeness of
perception and integrity of purpose not found among the mentally
unstable.

Apart from the fact that a mystical experience cannot be either
proved or disproved, the deeper problem, if she was merely a deluded
country girl, is to account for everything in Joan's life from the summer
of 1424 to her death. She did not claim her voices and visions in order
to cast herself as saintly or virtuous. In fact, as we have seen, she mentioned her experiences only to two confidants in the years before her
trial, and then she was hesitant to discuss the matter at all; true mystics are always reluctant to talk about themselves. Joan pointed not to
herself but to the cause and the challenge to which, she believed, God
summoned her and the French people: the salvation of the nation.

GEORGE BERNARD SHAW, who celebrated Joan in one of his most
famous plays, stated flatly that her voices represented plain common
sense. One might reply that common sense would have instructed her

to stay home, get on with her knitting, marry well, and raise a family—
all consistent with contemporary notions of female piety. Common
sense would not have impelled her to undertake a task that seemed
quixotic and perilous.

But Shaw was on the mark when he alluded to the relationship
between inspiration and imagination.

"I hear voices telling me what to do. They come from God," Joan
says in the play.

"They come from your imagination," replies Robert de Baudricourt,
military chief at Vaucouleurs.

"Of course," Joan retorts. "That is how the messages of God come
to us."

Of Joan's visions and voices, one thing must be emphasized. If they
came from the mind of a religious fanatic or a romantic, neurasthenic
adolescent, or if they were the specters of an inflamed mind or the
deliberately concocted tales of a self-deluded egotist, then we would
expect to find—would *have* to find—an accompanying pattern of delu-
sion in her life and a different set of circumstances than those that actually occurred. The delusions, hallucinations, or pleasant reveries would
be symptomatic of an unbalanced mind, or at least of an overactive fan-
tasist, and that lack of balance would have been revealed in her dealings
with family and friends, with princes and bishops, with soldiers and
with her accusers.

But instead of a delusional personality, we find a young woman of
remarkable composure, utterly refusing to seek the limelight. Not
much more than a peasant girl, she was convinced that she was summoned to a profoundly difficult task, to which she ultimately dedicated
herself despite all the logical reasons not to do so. Energetic, witty, courageous, and intelligent beyond all expectation, she showed an astonishing self-awareness that never tilted into vainglory. Even at her trial
she was hesitant to discuss her heavenly voices, and under duress her
statements often vary and are contradictory. That is not exceptional

when one is trying to preserve the integrity of a mysterious happening that occurred *interiorly* while being forced to discuss it before one's antagonists.

Now as then, many have tried to romanticize or to politicize Joan of Arc. But beyond all interpretations there remains the simple fact that against all odds she became a transforming presence in a world of male warriors, male royalty and male clergy, and she made it possible for France to resist absorption into the English empire. She altered the course of history by virtue of what might, at the least, be called an experience of heightened consciousness that provided a new direction for both her life and her world.

PEOPLE DO NOT have immediate experiences of God. Protracted and dramatic awareness of the Beyond is necessarily mediated through the terms and forms of one's culture; one might speak about "the voice of God" or the "voices of the angels." In the case of a genuine experience (which can be gauged, if not judged, only by its effects on the subject), it is important to note that throughout history those who do not engage in philosophical or theological discourse ordinarily experience the sublime in forms and terms familiar to them and readily available. It is the result of the experience that is new and that alters both perception and life.

One may have a more or less strong, direct and undeniable sense of the divine Presence, but this cannot be articulated or described without similes and metaphors; one feels at peace, it is said, or challenged or embraced; someone senses a new clarity or a new purpose. These words describe the effect of the experience, the psychospiritual reactions to it.

Something analogous occurred in the life of Francis of Assisi. A weary playboy and romantic dreamer without goals or ambition, he sought refuge from the summer heat in a cool, decrepit church one day in 1205, when he was twenty-three. Over the unused altar hung a striking image of the crucified Jesus, with painted eyes gazing directly and serenely toward the viewer. According to a contemporaneous account, "The image of Christ spoke to him in a tender and kind voice—'Francis, don't you see that my house is being destroyed? Go, then, and rebuild it for me.'" At that moment the young man took the words literally and began to clean up the forlorn church; only later did he understand there was a deeper injunction—to reform and rebuild the institutional Church itself.

The experiences of Francis and Joan were originally described in far less dramatic terms than some might wish. He heard a voice, as did she, and then did something about it. Joan heard an encouragement to prayer and fulfillment of her religious duties—and later she was commanded to help save France from extinction. But Joan and Francis told of the events in a calm, unhysterical, matter-of-fact manner, with nothing designed to advance themselves in the estimation of others. These were episodes in which two young people knew that they were touched and changed; after an initial period of confusion, they responded with action.

Many people, even those sympathetic to Francis and Joan, maintain that in a new age informed by depth psychology, such things as stated simply do not happen—but one might ask, "To *whom* do they not happen?" The lives of Francis of Assisi and Joan of Arc—indeed, the lives of Isaiah, Jesus of Nazareth, Buddha, and Muhammad—make little sense without reference to the world of the spirit, without reference to the living God, Who may disclose Himself as He wishes, to whom He wishes, under what circumstances He wishes. There is no sense in trying to stake a claim for Jesus, Francis, Joan or others as simply admirable humanitarians, patriots or social workers: their lives and deaths are too complex for such reduction. But if we agree that the mystery of Joan of Arc follows the tradition of those apprehended by the Beyond, we can appreciate the depths of her mystery. And that mystery is a living reality always capable of being freshly and more deeply comprehended.

History offers many such accounts of people being addressed by what might be called the world beyond—by a presence that could not be ignored. Moses before the burning bush; Isaiah awed by his vision of the majesty of God's court; Jesus aware of a profound sense of mission at the time of his baptism; the Buddha beholding the universe in a bouquet of flowers and Julian of Norwich seeing it in a hazelnut; the apostles Paul and John astonished by unexpected visions; Augustine hearing a child whisper, "Take up and read"—these moments revealed the intersection of the timeless with time, a conjunction of this world of sense and matter with another world.

It is important to remember that in each case the recipient never fully understands the experience and is forced to use the language of metaphor or poetry to communicate what is utterly transcendent. The ordinary limitations of language, which describe common experiences, have to be broken: there is, after all, no direct equivalent for an inner experience of such overwhelming power—invariably so overwhelming, in fact, that it alters one's perception of life and its purpose. Such was the experience of Joan of Arc.

THREE

Tomorrow, Not Later

(January 1428–February 1429)

From the beginning of her mystical experiences, Joan was neither impulsive nor complacent about them. For one thing, the precise nature of the call was made known to her only gradually. She also seemed to hesitate because she was unsure exactly how to respond and what reactions to expect from her parents, the local clergy and those conducting the war. She lived with her voices, pondering their meaning, praying about them and giving herself time to absorb the truth of them. It is astonishing just how stable and sensible she was in dealing with these extraordinary experiences.

A widespread misconception about Joan presumes that her patriotic fervor made her susceptible to a kind of autosuggestion—that her zeal, in other words, created the voices in her head. But the reverse was true: it was the voices that made her zealous for France. Another false impression is that she went very quickly—indeed, within days—from her quiet life in Domrémy to her role as warrior, mustering the troops and saving France. But the facts are quite otherwise: she began to hear voices and to see a great light in the summer of 1424, and for the next four years she remained at home, meditated on what was happening and continued to live (by all outward appearances) a normal life. During this time her voices revealed with increasing clarity the true nature of her vocation.

FINALLY, IN MAY 1428 her revelations were so lucid that she had to take action.* Joan had been inspired by her voices to approach Robert de Baudricourt, the captain of the military garrison at nearby Vaucouleurs, about ten miles north of Domrémy. Baudricourt, she hoped, would provide a military escort to the dauphin at Chinon.

The only women who attended or joined armies on maneuvers were prostitutes, "camp followers," and if Joan had told her parents of her intentions, they almost certainly would have locked her up. But as it happened, her mother's cousin, who lived near Vaucouleurs, was in the last months of pregnancy. Jeanne Laxart and her husband, Durand, resided in the village of Burey-le-Petit, and Joan was permitted to visit them. Once there, as Durand recalled, she helped with chores, "working around our house, spinning, helping in the garden, and looking after the animals.... She also asked me to go with her to Robert de Baudricourt." Joan must have been impressive and persuasive, for Durand did so.

With its crenellated fortifications and imposing castle, the walled town of Vaucouleurs had once been an appealing hilltop settlement overlooking the Meuse, but centuries of war left much of it decaying. Bertrand de Poulengy, an aristocrat, a squire and equerry of the king, was present for Joan's audience with Baudricourt. "She said she had come on behalf of the Lord," Poulengy testified later. "She asked Robert to tell the king to have patience, not to attack his enemies, and that the Lord would send help. She added most emphatically that the kingdom of France did not belong to the dauphin but to the Lord, who

---

* The historicity of the first journey to Vaucouleurs, in May 1428, is much debated, and some scholars insist there was but one trip, in early 1429. Despite the confusing evidence, the tradition of the earlier sojourn may be affirmed: in 1429, some at Vaucouleurs seem to have known her from a prior visit.

had given the country into the king's trust. Whereupon Robert asked who was this 'Lord' to whom Joan was referring, and she replied, 'the King of Heaven.'"

Baudricourt was unimpressed. Send a girl to join an army because she has a divine mandate? Nonsense. He told Laxart to give the girl a sound whipping and send her back to her father. By the end of May Joan had returned to Domrémy. Her parents apparently knew nothing about her visit to Vaucouleurs. And that, it seemed, was the end of that.

AT HOME ONCE again, Joan sought more opportunities for solitude. She engaged less frequently in the normal pastimes and activities of her peers, who recalled that she was no longer quite so gregarious or convivial. Although neither unapproachable nor impolite, she often slipped away from others and was later found praying in the family garden or in a nearby church. At least one of Joan's teenage companions presumed that the change in her personality indicated that she was about to marry, which would have been both legal and, at her age, anticipated by her family. Most girls were engaged by the age of twelve or thirteen and married soon after, with the encouragement of both Church and state; in 1428 Joan would have been sixteen.

About this time, Joan's parents made formal arrangements with a family who had an eligible son, to whom Joan was soon engaged. We know little of this episode in her life—neither the identity of the matrimonial match nor the precise date the ensuing fracas occurred. According to custom, the engagement did not require Joan's permission or approval; nor, it seems, was she introduced to her fiancé before the pact was settled. At the time, girls and young women took this procedure as a matter of course.

Legend has made Joan an attractive young woman, but norms of appeal shift with time and culture. Renaissance Europe prized women with opulent figures; centuries later a malnourished look rules the world of fashion. In late medieval France there was no single standard of judgment. That said, can we know anything of Joan's appearance?

A sketch by a notary, from a 1429 document about the battle at Orléans, shows in the margin a plain girl with long hair and an elaborate gown alongside a mention of the Maid. But there is no proof that the doodler ever saw her, and in any case Joan did not go into battle wearing an ornate coiffeur and decorative dress. Several of her companions-at-arms described her as a comely young woman with an appealing figure. Apart from that, there are no verbal or visual images of Joan from her lifetime, and subsequent miniatures, paintings, and statues only forced her to conform to prevalent fashions.

Over the centuries the most repeated representations of Joan have cast her as shepherdess or as a soldier; in the latter depictions she is absurdly shown wearing a robe over her armor, as if her gender would otherwise be questioned. In late nineteenth-century advertising, however, she was a radiantly healthy provincial schoolgirl, and by the time of her canonization in 1920 Joan of Arc variously resembled a model, a silent movie star, an idealized university student, or a challenger in the women's Olympics.

WHATEVER HER APPEARANCE, Joan was no ordinary teenager. Regarding her engagement, the little that survived on the record is so unusual as to be shocking for its time: she repudiated her parents' wishes and declined the deal they had made with the boy and his family. Because the agreement to marry was a legal covenant, Joan was sued for breach of contract. Canon law, however, requires a free assent of the will in order to validate a marriage, and because that was lacking, the sacrament of matrimony could not be performed. The local bishop dismissed the case in Joan's favor, and the rejected suitor receded into the mists of oblivion whence he had briefly emerged. This was, Joan later said, the only time she disobeyed her parents.

Although it was unknown at that time, there was a good reason for Joan's firm rejection of marriage. She saw ever more clearly that her summons to act on behalf of France would require her to remain single—and not simply unmarried, but chaste by vow.

Joan saw her mission as a religious calling. At that time it was not unusual for an unmarried man or woman to make a private vow of chastity; that had long been a hallowed tradition in Christian piety, for it demonstrated one's willingness to accept a particular task from God by a total consecration of body and soul.

There is no evidence, however, that Joan saw her vow as perpetual; her private promise was to remain chaste "as long as it should be pleasing to God." She was, in other words, unique in another way: she was dedicating herself neither as a nun nor as a laywoman associated with a religious community (like Catherine of Siena). She saw her virginity as a corollary of the imminent task to which she freely responded. The terms of her promise ("as long as …") implied that, should God lead her along other paths in the future, she would be open to His plan for her to marry and bear children. This idea that a vow could be temporary, and that one's vocation might later be altered by circumstances, was not typical of the time. But Joan trusted God to lead her along the right paths at the right time, regardless of her own expectations. Indeed, she was no ordinary teenager.

For the present, then, she would have no husband, and she would guard her virginity against every effort of male charms. It should be added that there is nothing in her life to suggest that she had a pathological revulsion toward men; on the contrary, the details of her military expeditions indicate that she had healthy friendships with men and collaborated with them in an open and mature manner. She was, in other words, not intimidated by men, whether they were soldiers or bishops.

Nor is there any indication that she was repelled by the idea of sex. That would be a retrojected suspicion, based on the widespread later presumption that every sane woman marries, has romantic affairs, or is ready to tangle in easy sexual liaisons. But not all women act according to such (mostly male) expectations and preconceptions.

JOAN WAS BREAKING the mold in yet another way. The cloister was the ordinary choice for a devout woman who wished to dedicate herself to God.* This meant a life of total enclosure as a vowed nun, entirely removed from the world; active religious congregations of teaching and nursing sisters flourished only later. There is no evidence that Joan ever intended to be a nun or even that she knew one. That made her vow all the more anomalous.

The primacy of the cloister, held before medieval girls as the highest ideal to which they could aspire, has interesting historic roots. For almost all of its first three centuries, Christianity was illegal in the Roman Empire, and martyrdom became the ultimate act of fidelity to Jesus Christ. After the emperor Constantine made Christianity the official religion in the fourth century, martyrdom was replaced by vowed chastity, by fasting, and by other forms of physical self-denial. Groups of women and men in the Eastern and North African deserts, then in Asia Minor, the Holy Land, Gaul and the rest of the empire, formed eremitical communities, always far from cities.

Unfortunately, for all its great contribution to the literature of prayer and mystical experience, such a flight from the world eventually led to the distorted and unorthodox notion that the material world and all things to do with the body were inherently evil and had to be avoided or at least held in contempt. Such a view spread outward from the des-

* As late as the thirteenth century, two hundred years before Joan, Clare of Assisi was forced into a convent. She had wanted to live like her friend Francis, dedicated but in the world. The regulations of the time, however, required him to put her in an enclosure. A century after Clare, Catherine of Siena was one of the first egregious exceptions to this tradition.

ert monks to all the faithful, and it is clearly antithetical to the basis of Christian faith itself, with its belief that God has embraced the world and all its materiality. This attitude of distrust and even hatred of the world persisted and flourished in medieval life; thus chastity, like the abandonment of personal wealth, was regarded as a most honorable estate, and the traditional place in which to lead an angelic, chaste life was the convent or monastic community.

If a woman did not choose consecrated virginity, Church and society ordinarily expected her to marry and bear as many children as possible. The Church would thus have more loyal adherents, and society would have more hands to work the farms; additionally, people were encouraged to repopulate Christian Europe after the ravages of the plague. In such a culture, the child was seen as a producer, not a consumer. Catherine of Siena's mother bore twenty-five children, and her condition of unremitting pregnancy was regarded as extremely admirable (and, perhaps by some of her neighbors, a bit overzealous).

It was logical for Joan to live chastely "as long as it should be pleasing to God," the better to commit everything of herself to Him without reservation. "I must keep the promise I made to Our Lord, to keep my virginity of body and soul." That is the essential key to what might otherwise be regarded as mere continence. Like others who consecrated their lives outside convents and monasteries, Joan would be autonomous but nevertheless entirely dependent on God.

To keep her virginity meant to rely on God, to abandon herself to His mercies, and not to rely on herself or a man, her motives or his, her actions or talents or his. This abandonment, this absolute trust in God, lies at the core of all Christian spirituality; it is also the incontrovertible mark of authentic prayer. It does not imply inactivity or passivity: it is the mark of a life that gives up trust in self in order to give that self over to God. At this point Joan began to identify herself as "la Pucelle"—the maid, the virgin. Of course, there are many other ways for consecration of self to God besides vowed virginity, but this was Joan's way.

Her chaste condition was her identity, and this derived from the sense of self provided by her revelations. As Joan's contemporary Thomas Basin, the bishop of Lisieux, wrote not long after her death:

Regarding her mission, and the apparitions and revelations that she said she had, everyone has the right to believe as he pleases, to reject them or not, according to his point of view or way of thinking. What is important regarding these visions is the fact that Joan had herself no shadow of a doubt regarding their reality, and it was their effect upon her, and not her natural inclination, that impelled her to leave her parents and her home to undertake great perils and to endure great hardships—and, as it proved, a terrible death. It was these visions and voices, and they alone, which enabled her to believe that she would succeed in saving her country and in placing her king on his throne. It was these visions and voices which finally enabled her to do those marvelous deeds, and accomplish what appeared to all the world as impossible.

IN JULY 1428, life changed dramatically for Joan and her family. On their way to attack Vaucouleurs and thus destroy the major northern center supporting the Valois, the Burgundians pillaged the towns surrounding Domrémy. Jacques, Isabelle, and their children quickly gathered what possessions and livestock they could and with some of their neighbors fled for refuge to the fortified town of Neufchâteau, five miles south. There they lodged at a small inn owned by a woman nicknamed *la rousse*, "the redhead." For several weeks Joan and her mother helped with the serving and household chores. When the family at last returned to Domrémy, they saw that armed horsemen had plundered and burned the local church, laid waste most of the fields and homes, and attacked the women who could not flee.

And then an ominous report reached them through mendicant friars and couriers passing through on their way to Vaucouleurs. In October the English army, under the command of the Earl of Salisbury, besieged Orléans, the last major city loyal to the Valois. Within a fortnight the town was encircled and soldiers destroyed the bridge linking it to territory controlled by the dauphin. The invaders planned to starve Orléans of food and all necessary supplies. The formal accession and anointing of the dauphin as king were thus in immediate and grave jeopardy, for Chinon would fall after Orléans, and young Charles VII with it.

Joan and her family must have been enraged and all the more determined to resist the partisans of England. It would have been natural if her father and brothers, along with some neighbors, were roused to speak of joining the forces in support of the dauphin. But how could they do that, and where could they fight? How could they withstand so well armed an enemy, who swept down on them like a sudden storm? Joan herself may have joined in such conversations, saying she too wanted to do something—anything—to help the French cause.

We cannot be certain of such talk, but we do know that her father was suddenly suspicious of her intentions. As a trial note states, "Her mother told her that her father had dreamed of Joan going off with men of arms, and so her parents were insistent on keeping a watch over her. Her father said to her brothers, 'If I thought that my dream was coming true, I'd want you to drown her—and if you didn't, I'd do it myself.'" The reason for his violent reaction to the dream was obvious. A girl "going off with men of arms" could mean only one thing—that she was setting out as a camp follower, a prostitute.

After Christmas, without telling family or friends, Joan walked the ten-mile distance to Vaucouleurs, intending to confront the captain on her own, to obtain his recommendation of her to the dauphin, and to plead for an escort for her journey to Chinon. She bade farewell to no one, neither family nor friends, doubtless expecting them to imagine that she had returned to her cousins to help after the baby's birth.

When they learned her true whereabouts and her purpose, Joan's parents were angry and frightened; later they were reconciled to her.

This time Joan stayed with friends of the Laxarts, a family named Le Royer, and from there she went again to beg an audience with the commander of the fortress. Finally her sheer persistence was rewarded.

FOR SEVERAL GENERATIONS Robert de Baudricourt's family had fought resolutely against the English occupation of France. Although some accounts characterize him as rude and dissolute, Baudricourt finally listened to Joan and admired her zeal for the Valois crown. Despite the opinion of advisers who urged him to dismiss her permanently, Baudricourt did not: he temporized, without passing judgment on her visions and voices. On the matter of sending her directly to the dauphin, however, he refused. But Joan sensed that this rebuff was not quite so firm and fixed. This time she did not return to Domrémy but remained in Vaucouleurs with the Royers. Jean le Fumeux, an altar boy and later a curate at the local church of Notre-Dame des Voûtes, recalled seeing Joan at Mass there every day that January.

Then, toward the end of that month, things began to happen quickly.

Baudricourt felt that he could not endorse Joan's plan or trust her claims to divine guidance unless he had some collegial support for her. His close friend René of Anjou, son-in-law of Charles, Duke of Lorraine, had grown up with the dauphin. Baudricourt and René exchanged letters, and one morning a messenger arrived at the Royer cottage. Joan was summoned to travel to the town of Nancy in Lorraine, where she was to meet the duke, then sixty-four and very ill. If she were truly sent by God, Joan was told, she would be able to cure Charles by some miraculous means.

With safe conduct provided by Baudricourt, Joan went at once to the duke's residence in Nancy (thirty miles from Vaucouleurs, a day's horseback ride); Durand Laxart accompanied her, along with one or two of Baudricourt's squires. Ushered into the presence of the ailing duke, Joan was asked to perform a miracle on his behalf. She told him that she had no control over his illness and well-being—and in any case, she added with extraordinary sangfroid, the duke ought to regain his character more zealously than his vigor. Accordingly, she advised him to give up his mistress and take back his wife. "She then said that she would pray to God for his health." In spite of himself, Charles of Lorraine was duly impressed and gave Joan money for the journey she had undertaken to visit him.

Back in Vaucouleurs, Joan was teased by one of Baudricourt's loyal companions and squires, Jean de Metz: "*M'amie* ["Sweetheart" or "Honey," here used ironically], what are you doing here? Shouldn't the dauphin be thrown out, and then we'll all become English?"

"I'm here," Joan replied, "to ask Robert de Baudricourt's help in going to the king—but he pays no attention to me. I must save France, even though I would prefer to stay home and spin wool with my mother, for this sort of thing is not my proper station in life. But I must go, because my Lord wills that I do so."

"And who is your Lord?"

"God," she answered.

Jean de Metz, then about twenty-nine, teased her no more. "I put my hand in hers as a sign of good faith," he said years later, "and I promised to do all I could to lead her to the king." By placing his hand between her two hands—the formal gesture of knightly loyalty—Metz effectively became Joan's liege man, her follower in faithful service. With that, Joan began to attract loyalty and inspire confidence among both the townsfolk and some men in Baudricourt's retinue, including Bertrand de Poulengy, who had been present at her first audience with Baudricourt. Up to this point the captain of Vaucouleurs and his advisers thought the girl in the tattered country-russet skirt (*pauvres vêtements de femmes, rouges*, according to Jean de Metz) had a quixotic goal indeed; now they were no longer so sure.

Meantime Baudricourt sent a message to Chinon by way of his courier, Colet de Vienne, asking if Joan would be admitted should he decide to send her for their consideration. With the dauphin's financial and military fortunes in full ruin, he had little to lose, as a clerk replied. They could send the girl along, and they would see what they would see.

But there was one final examination to which the captain wished to subject the Maid. To the Royer home came Baudricourt himself, accompanied by a priest. As Madame Le Royer recalled, a kind of medieval ordeal ensued, although a nonviolent one. The clergyman put a liturgical stole around his neck and took up a cross. He told Joan that if she was indeed inhabited by a good spirit she must approach him and kneel, and if she harbored a devil she must forthwith quit the house. This was a routine intended to carry out a discernment of spirits. Testily Joan replied that this procedure was neither necessary nor appropriate: the priest had several times heard her confession at the local church, and he knew the state of her soul. Still, she did as she was told and reverently knelt before him.

By now Baudricourt was under pressure from the people of Vaucouleurs and his own entourage, almost all of whom were favorably impressed with Joan's integrity, piety, and clarity—and unlike the mercenaries who comprised the army, she was a volunteer. And so the captain began to make arrangements for her journey to Chinon.

FOR HUNDREDS OF years in Europe, groups of country folk had been leaving their homes to be of service elsewhere, persuaded that one critical situation or another required them to redress injustice or go to the aid of those in need. From the eleventh century, for example, groups who called themselves les pauvres—poor in spirit if not always in pocketbook—and those called pueri, or servants, had undertaken pilgrimages. A misreading of pueri, which also meant "boys," inspired the false idea that children were conscripted into the Crusades; on the contrary, the *pueri* of those tragic expeditions were, both literally and symbolically, servants, often but not always also *pauvres*.

For her journey to Chinon, a major alteration had to be made in Joan's outward appearance. She could hardly ride hundreds of miles on horseback wearing the now-threadbare red skirt she had brought from Domrémy. This was first pointed out to her by Jean de Metz, who asked her if she intended to continue wearing her own clothes. She at once saw the impracticality of them and replied no, she would rather have a man's riding outfit. "And so I gave her some of my own young servants' clothes and boots," Metz continued, adding that Bertrand de Poulengy and some townspeople supplemented this with "everything necessary for the journey." They also shared the cost of her horse. Baudricourt gave her a sword, and a linen banner or standard was made for her to carry, the better to be seen. Later it was sewn with a pattern of fleur-de-lis, two angels and the names "Jesus Maria" along the side.

The Maid now had the proper riding clothes. So attired, she looked like a mounted page: her hair was cropped short under a leather hood, and a belt cinched her short coat, beneath which she wore underpants, a doublet (an undercoat padded with a solid breastplate), and a shirt and hose that were attached to the doublet with hooks. With boots, spurs, and a short cape for warmth, her outfit was complete.

The practical necessity of such a wardrobe had another purpose. Because she was going to be constantly in the company of men, she had to dress like one, for protection. Her clothes had to conceal or at least deemphasize her gender, thus to protect her from rape by Burgundians, attack by mere highwaymen they might encounter en route, and even assault by her own allies. A practical soul, she saw no reason not to wear sensible clothes. In modern times some radical analysts have insisted that Joan's male wardrobe indicates that she was either a transvestite or a lesbian. If that skewed judgment is correct, then every woman who wears, for example, overalls for work or sport or a riding

habit or even elegant trousers ought to be similarly charged as residing
on the margins of "normal" sexuality.

As for the idea that a woman was forbidden by biblical and ecclesiastical law from wearing men's clothes under any and every circumstance,
that was simply not so: women were encouraged to adopt a disguise
when necessary—for instance, to protect themselves. However, a
woman was not permitted to live every day of her life cross-dressed as a
man and intending to be taken for a man, for that would be to imitate
what was presumed to be the loftier status of men. The townspeople of
Vaucouleurs thought as did Joan: the change of clothing was merely
expedient, and there was no discussion about it; later, however, her
male clothing became the overriding argument for her execution.

When her accoutrements were in order, Jean de Metz asked Joan
when she would like to head for Chinon. "Tomorrow rather than
later," she replied, "but even better, now."

JOAN DEPARTED ON Wednesday, February 23. Henri Le Royer came
to the town square to say good-bye, expressing his concern about her
safety among soldiers, brigands and Burgundians. "She was not afraid
[Le Royer recalled], for she had God, her Lord, Who would clear the
road for her to go to the dauphin. She said she was born for this." Robert de Baudricourt uttered an ambiguous farewell, directed, in the singular imperative, to Joan: "*Va, et advienne que pourra.* Go, and come
what may." In a sense, he was washing his hands of Joan and her campaign, and he was doubtless relieved to see her depart. He had done his
duty, he had tried to discourage her, he had tested her spirit. The whole
enterprise seemed hopelessly unrealistic to this gruff, pessimistic commander.

Joan had an entourage of six: Jean de Metz and his servant; Bertrand
de Poulengy and his attendant; Colet de Vienne, a royal messenger who
knew the route; and a Scottish archer named Richard, a mercenary.

Metz and Poulengy provided food and supplies and bore the expenses of the journey, including payments to the other men; the money for Joan's horse was raised by the townsfolk. With the blessing of the local priest and the cheers of a crowd, the group rode down the hillside.*
The day was frigid, the earth hard as iron, the sun obscured behind wintry clouds.

As Saint Benedict had enjoined, abbeys traditionally offered hospitality to travelers. The superior of the monastery of Saint-Urbain was a relative of Baudricourt, and he went out to greet the sojourners from Vaucouleurs on the first night of their journey, when (as Poulengy recalled) they stopped "for fear of the Burgundians who were numerous in the region." The men slept in the monastery; Joan was lodged in a guest cottage, as women routinely were.

The remaining itinerary took them through Clairvaux, Pothières, Mezilles, Saint-Aignan and L'Ile-Bouchard. "During our journey, Joan used to say it would be good for all of us if we could attend Mass," added Metz, "but we were afraid of being recognized [as French loyalists], and so we went to Mass only twice"—at Auxerre and Saint-Catherine-de-Fierbois, towns sympathetic to the dauphin.

Chinon was a distance of about three hundred fifty miles, and Colet de Vienne calculated a journey of eleven to twelve days, barring fierce weather or attack. At first they thought their hardy young lady might be more than foolish; Joan was sincere, but they wondered if she might not also be a bit mad. They were soon disabused of this suspicion and recognized that her single-mindedness was a sign of fidelity to a calling far beyond the political.

Poulengy was about thirty-six and Metz about thirty—and they were both, as Bertrand put it, "young and strong," which then implied sexual health and responsiveness, as he confirmed in his remarks

---

* That Joan could ride well would not have been unusual: the horse was the usual method of transport, and, like her peers, she would have ridden her father's animals in Domrémy from an early age.

following: "At night Joan slept close to Jean de Metz and me—but without ever removing her coat, doublet, hose, or boots. I was young and strong, but I wouldn't have dared touch her, because of the goodness I saw in her." Jean agreed, as he too later said in sworn testimony: "She was right beside us at night, but she inspired such respect that I wouldn't have dared to make any advance. On my oath, I tell you that there was no carnal movement toward her—I was so much inspired by her words and by her love of God. Very soon I came to believe that she was indeed sent by God Himself."

It is important to recall that in times past an obviously pious woman would have been shown respect and chivalric admiration. In fact there was a kind of restraining, knightly scruple against taking advantage of her (which, in Joan's case, her clothing would have made difficult but not impossible if men became sufficiently violent). Joan's goodness, in other words, did not make her seem a greater challenge to their seductive skills. After Joan's death Poulengy testified that he had never seen in her "the slightest evidence of any wickedness or sin; she was really so good that, even then, we could have called her a saint."

ON THURSDAY, MARCH 3, they stopped at Saint-Catherine-de-Fierbois, a village ten miles east of Chinon, named for the legendary martyr who was one of Joan's spiritual patrons. After Mass they dined, and then Joan dictated a letter to her parents, asking pardon for whatever heartache she may have caused by her precipitous departure. Her mother and father forgave her and sent a private chaplain to attend her on her mission; in addition, her brothers, Pierre and Jean, left Domrémy at once to join her. At the same time, Joan sent word to the dauphin, formally seeking permission to enter Chinon and adding that she had many good things to tell him.

Traveling as cautiously and covertly as possible, the group arrived without incident at Chinon about midday on Friday, March 4—a day or two ahead of their estimate, thanks to their high energy and the favorable weather. The journey had been without misadventure; now Joan only had to await her introduction to the man she referred to as "my king." Meantime, she and her escorts lodged at an inn, and two royal counselors were sent to evaluate Joan and report back to the court.

"They put a lot of questions to her," recalled Jean de Metz. One of the king's men thought she was quite deranged; the other, touched by the sincerity of Joan's claim that she had been sent by God, advised Charles to grant her an audience. At the same time, the king received another message from Robert de Baudricourt, which, while not exactly endorsing Joan, stated plainly that she had seemed to everyone in Vaucouleurs a pious and brave Maid. This letter was perhaps intended to protect himself in case the king was disappointed in Joan—as if he were writing, "This isn't *my* opinion, of course, but people seemed to like her...."

Finally, on Sunday, March 6, Joan was invited to court. But a group of cavaliers, wary of anyone who might supplant their own influence with Charles, told him that she had claimed supernatural powers as a wonder-worker. To prove it, the courtiers said, Joan ought to do something quite remarkable. Hence an elaborate experiment was devised.

FOUR

Armor and a Household

(March–April 1429)

In 1429 the three massive sections of the castle of Chinon—300,000 square feet of thick-walled fortress—still towered over the ancient town and the forests and vineyards of Touraine. Built over several centuries on the site of an ancient Roman camp, the chateau also dominated the riverbanks of the Vienne, a tributary of the Loire.

Within its walls the uncrowned and dispirited young king had taken refuge with a court that was clutching at straws. The English commanded Paris, Reims, and most of the country north of the Loire; Orléans was about to collapse. A cadre of devious advisers did Charles no good, and his war treasury was virtually empty. But most worrisome of all was the rumor that Charles's mother had said he might be illegitimate—a slur that, if she uttered it, she knew was untrue; it was, however, enough to make both Charles and some powerful ducal allies doubt the legitimacy of his claim to the crown. And although a significant number of the people supported him, the king had little help from the wealthy nobility, from whom he always needed financial support.

Often indifferent, sometimes sad, and always indecisive, the young Charles was in private a temperate and pious man, but he had to provide luxuries for his hedonistic courtiers and self-indulgent aristocrats.

Discerning witnesses, however, recognized his weariness and disgust with both the war and himself. In 1429 Charles VII was only twenty-six, but he was remarkably spiritless. Jean Fouquet's picture of him, completed during Charles's lifetime, shows a homely, sad, and distracted man of no great appeal, but that is how Fouquet represented all his subjects, male and female. By contrast, almost all contemporary writers remarked on Charles's agreeable, even handsome, appearance.

Charles was as ill served by many contemporary chroniclers as he was by portraitists. The historical record shows that he was certainly not the ineffective character of English record. He hated war and he was often lacking self-confidence, but he was eventually one of the most effective sovereigns of the late Middle Ages.

For several reasons he did not expect to inherit the throne of France. Born in 1403, he was the eleventh child and fifth son of Charles VI and Isabeau of Bavaria. Surrounded in his early years by the madness of his father and the deaths of siblings, he was then raised by the mother of Marie d'Anjou, a nine-year-old girl to whom, by arrangement, he was engaged when he was only ten; this alliance later provided him with the enormous political influence of the house of Anjou. Subsequently, his older brothers died, and he found himself in direct line to wear the crown. Thin, physically weak, suspicious, and insecure, Charles seemed at first an unlikely monarch.

Much of his anxiety derived from the event that had occurred when he was sixteen—when Jean, Duke of Burgundy, was assassinated by Charles's partisans (almost certainly with at least his tacit consent), and the Treaty of Troyes turned the throne of France over to the descendants of Henry V, thus denying it to young Charles. By the time the mad Charles VI died in 1422, he had officially disinherited his surviving son, who nevertheless continued to insist on his legacy, only to see it disputed both by the English and by many French.

Less than two months after his father's death, the dauphin married Marie d'Anjou. At the same time he inherited a country that was, as the Burgundian chronicler Georges Chastellain lamented, "turned upside down, a footstool for mankind, the winepress of the English, and a doormat for brigands." A peacemaker at heart, Charles wanted to pursue concord at home and abroad: he had an intense dislike for hostility, much less violent warfare. Cultivated, multilingual, and intellectually sophisticated, he was a fascinating combination of piety, learning, and compassion counterpoised by anxiety, vacillation, and a deep desire for solitude. In his early years as king he seemed, in fact, to regret his ancestry and what it had forced on him.

Making matters worse for Charles was his financial dilemma: taxes were insufficient for him to wage war successfully, and he had to borrow prodigiously from nobles and financiers. Unfortunately, he had only a motley band of ragtag, undisciplined mercenaries for an army, and for the most part the king could afford to pay them only about a third of their contracted allowance. Additionally, the royal military commanders were little better than bandits, and many of them were hired from Italy, Spain, and Scotland. The English militia found it almost easy to defeat them in battle after battle, from 1423 up to the siege of Orléans in 1429, and Charles's constant attempts to end the war by seeking reconciliation with Burgundy were stymied by the memory of the old duke's murder. By the time Joan arrived on the scene, according to one source, he was discouraged and disgusted; he considered giving everything up to the English and retiring to Spain. Just such a confused and confusing man awaited Joan that day.

EARLY DURING THE evening of Sunday, March 6, the Maid and her companions rode up the steep approach and across a drawbridge to the castle, which was comprised of three fortresses linked by bridges. At that moment a widely reported incident occurred. As Joan was about to dismount, a man, also on horseback, reined in her steed. "Isn't this the famous maid from Vaucouleurs?" he asked, adding with a lascivious sneer: "If I could have you for one night, you wouldn't be a maiden any more!" The anecdote concludes with Joan scolding him for such conduct and warning him that he was near death—an event that apparently occurred within the hour.

Joan was escorted into the Great Hall; seventy feet long and thirty-three feet wide, it was packed with more than three hundred courtiers, friends, and supporters of the dauphin. And then the carefully planned ruse was set in motion. Charles had put off his royal finery and was dressed like an ordinary citizen, surrounded by others, with nothing to suggest his identity. If Joan was all that she was rumored to be, then her purity of heart should enable her to detect the king of France amid a vast throng. This was a standard test of spiritual discernment.

Joan approached Charles straightaway, not at all intimidated by the august gathering. Many of Joan's partisans then and later took this as another miracle, but that may be an unnecessary interpretation. She may well have been told about the ruse in advance, or someone may have described the king to her. In any case, her discovery of him is not as critical as what then occurred.

By their side that evening was a chamberlain and knight of the dauphin named Raoul de Gaucourt, who was also governor of Orléans and thus responsible for shoring up its defenses. Years later he clearly recalled Joan's words: "My most eminent lord Dauphin, I have come, sent by God, to bring help to you and to the kingdom."[*] It was as direct and unadorned a summary as the dauphin—and anyone else before or since—could ask. Help for him and for France: that was her message and her vocation.

Joan spoke with such quiet conviction, and so undramatic and unadorned was her reference to being "sent by God" that she was difficult to ignore. At that time, claims to bear a mandate from God were not

---

[*] Some sources amplify the incident with extended dialogue, the better to dramatize the first meeting between Joan and Charles.

rejected out of hand: they were tested, doubted, challenged—but not forthwith dismissed as inauthentic. The medieval mind took for granted that just as God had done in the great events of revelation from Abraham through Jesus, so He continued to act in the world through human agency. From that moment in the Great Hall, Charles was fascinated by the seventeen-year-old girl who stood calmly and confidently before him.

He then took Joan aside for a few moments, and after a brief but apparently intense private conversation, he seemed to one member of his court to be "radiant." At Joan's trial—and in countless works since then—many speculated about the content of that discussion, which neither she nor the dauphin ever disclosed. Did Joan impart a specific revelation from her voices? Perhaps, for at her trial she insisted that she shared the nature of her mystical experiences only with Baudricourt and the king. But precisely what was the content of the revelation she shared? Moments before, she had told Charles the reason for her presence in Chinon, and that did not make him "radiant."

Or did Joan perhaps reveal something about Charles himself that only he could have known, thus demonstrating that she was God's good servant, a girl with exceptional spiritual insight? That is possible too, and many endorse this—except that Joan (and the God she served) seems not to have gone for mere sideshow tricks. Scholars and hagiographers have wondered and placed their bets about this episode, and they continue to do so. But every opinion is mere hypothesis. Perhaps it is best to accept that in their chat, Joan's faith and determination infused new hope and confidence into this hitherto indecisive, fearful young man.

WHATEVER THEY DISCUSSED in private, Charles acted at once. First, he asked that Joan be transferred from the local inn and reside as his guest, in a part of the chateau called the tower of Couldray (or Coudray), which had a chapel nearby. The dauphin also assigned a page, a personal aide, to be taken from Gaucourt's retinue and charged with her security. His name was Louis de Coutes, he was about fifteen years old and he became a loyal and respectful presence in the months to come.* Of Joan's time at the castle, Louis later said, "I was continuously with her during the day. At night she had women with her [for protection]. And I recall that while she was there, men of high rank came to see her several times."

Among them, none was more prestigious or sympathetic than Jean, Duke of Alençon, a duchy in northwestern France. Then twenty-three, he was a handsome, intelligent and courteous man, a close friend of the king and godfather to his son. Jean had been a prisoner of the English for five years, since his capture at the battle of Verneuil in 1424, when he was seventeen. He had been set free only two weeks before he met Joan, when at last the ransom offered by his wife, Jeanne, was accepted by his captors; she pawned all her jewelry to gain his release.

Jean was enjoying his emancipation by hunting quail when Charles sent word to him about Joan. At once the duke rode to Chinon, where he found her talking with Charles. "She asked me who I was," Alençon recalled, "and then she said to me, 'You are very welcome. The more people we have who share the blood of France, the better it will be.'" This meeting, on Monday, March 7, began a lifelong friendship between Joan and the man she always called "my fair Duke."

Next day Joan, Jean and the king dined together, and afterward the duke and the Maid jousted for sport. "Seeing her manage her lance so well, I gave her a horse," Alençon recalled. This steed replaced the one she had ridden from Vaucouleurs.

Over the next two days Charles asked for the impressions of several bishops and priests. "They interrogated her in my presence," according

---

* Mark Twain's fictional biography, *Personal Recollections of Joan of Arc* (1895), is narrated by a character named Sieur Louis de Conte, a variant of the name of Joan's real-life page. His initials (S.L.C.) are also, of course, the initials of Twain's real name, Samuel Langhorne Clemens.

to Alençon, "asking why she had come. She replied that she had come from the King of Heaven, that she heard voices and counsel that told her what she was to do. Later she told me that she could do much more than she had told them." Joan replied to the queries as briefly as possible and without elaborating on her spiritual experience; for her, the focus was France, not Joan.

But patience was not among her virtues. Eager for the liberation of Orléans, she reminded her interrogators that the blockade was causing enormous suffering and augured the most critical time for the dauphin's survival; and the English were making daily advances even as the French were losing ground. In the spirit of Baudricourt, however, her examiners considered Joan naive and impractical, but they found nothing offensive or irreligious in her words or claims; to the contrary, they found admirable her devotion to the cause of France.

The questions continued from Tuesday through Thursday, March 8 to 10. Alençon saw that Joan was becoming annoyed by this delay and growing intolerant of the clergymen's repetitious discourse. The dauphin too noticed her slight edginess: she gave the impression that she had not come all the way from Domrémy and Vaucouleurs to submit to a theological examination. But rather than taking offense at her ardor, Charles had to admire both her poise and her urgency in the presence of these robed and learned men.

At this point something quite remarkable emerges about Joan of Arc.

In her time, clergymen in general and bishops in particular were held in almost mystic regard by ordinary people and by kings and princes. This was not always a sign of piety or even superstition: such obvious reverence was required if one were to obtain the political support of the Church. As in the presence of secular princes, people knelt and kissed the hands and rings of bishops. In England bishops and noblemen were called "my lord," the same address as in France, where each was "*mon seigneur*." An attack on a priest was cause for excommunication, and the murder of any cleric brought swift execution. More to the point, the clergy often received a degree of deference that was nearly idolatrous and certainly theologically indefensible.

Joan was no young rebel, nor did she set herself against the authority or expertise of prelates. But she knew what she knew, and no ecclesiastical orator ever bullied or overawed her. In this regard she always pointed to the unassailable truth of her voices and visions—to the primacy of her conscience, although she never would have used those modern words.

Joan believed that God had addressed her and entrusted her with the task of liberating Orléans, and she could neither deny nor suppress that experience any more than she could read a letter or translate a document from one language to another. Even had she been able, Joan felt no compulsion to answer the convoluted questions of prelates with clever or high-toned academic replies. With the apostle Paul, she could have insisted, "I am not ashamed—I know the One in whom I believe." Indeed, her actions spoke for her.

THERE REMAINED A final delay—a much longer one, as it happened, although (like her interrogators at Chinon) the questioners, all of them loyal to Charles, were neither hostile nor contemptuous. On Friday, March 11, she was sent on a thirty-mile journey south to Poitiers; there Joan was further examined by a board of theologians charged to confirm her probity and to assure that her views were congruent with (or at least not contradictory to) Church teaching. In addition, her claims to divine inspiration had to be supported by an honorable life and a miraculous sign—which of course was to be the liberation of Orléans, still a future event.

Friar Séguin, a Dominican professor, was among the benevolent examiners. "She spoke in a most dignified manner," he recalled, and she said "that a voice told her that God had great pity on the people of France, and that she must go to Vaucouleurs, where she would find a captain who would enable her to go to the king." Séguin's impression coincided with that of Albert d'Ourches, a local *seigneur*, who had said, "I would have been very pleased to have so good a daughter as she."

Something of Joan's humor and spirit comes through in Séguin's recollections about the examination at Poitiers that March. When he asked her what language her voices spoke, she referred to his native dialect (actually quite distinct from French) and replied, "Better than yours!" Séguin then asked if Joan believed in God: "Better than you!" was her lively riposte. Her impatience made her feisty, and the professors found her mettle refreshing. Asked for a sign—a miracle or a dramatic proof of her godliness—she replied, "In the name of God: I did not come to Poitiers to produce signs." She paused and then stared at them gravely: "Lead me to Orléans, and I will show you the sign." The miracle would be the liberation, which she was certain God would provide.

The record of the two-week interrogation does not survive but for the recollections of a few people almost thirty years later. But the conclusion of the examiners does, and its recommendation to the king is rather muted:

> The king should not reject the maid who says that God has sent her to bring him help, even though those promises and their fulfillment may lie in a completely natural realm. On the other hand, the king should not be too credulous about the maid, either.... [However,] no evil has been found in her, only goodness, humility, virginity and devotion, honesty and simplicity. Now seeing that the king finds no evil in her either, and aware of her urgent request to be sent to Orléans—to show that indeed she is the bearer of divine aid—the king should not hinder her from going to Orléans with soldiers. Rather, he should send her there forthwith, trusting God. To fear or reject her would be to rebel against the Holy Spirit and to render oneself unworthy of divine aid.

In this report no mention is made of what has been presumed to be
the further reason for Joan's campaign—to see that Charles would be
duly anointed king at Reims. In fact, at this point in her life Joan seems
to have had only the liberation of Orléans in mind, and just so much
may have been revealed to her. If this is so, then only in light of her
subsequent success at Orléans was she encouraged (by her voices and
perhaps by the king's council) to escort Charles to his coronation. God
addressed her progressively, in other words, through her voices and
through events—and these had spoken to her only gradually; after all,
how much could she be expected to absorb all at once? The revelations,
like the history of salvation in the Scriptures, were progressive, and her
spiritual life was a process. In fact, it may be difficult to accept otherwise: surely God's plan could be disclosed to her (as to anyone) only in
stages.

Others urged the king to take Joan very seriously indeed. Jacques
Gélu held the ancient and prestigious archbishopric of Embrun, located
in the High Alps about fifteen miles from the Italian border. Learned,
cautious and devout, he urged Charles to take care lest he be tricked by
Joan, an ignorant peasant girl; still, he recommended that she be treated with the utmost courtesy and that her claims be earnestly considered. Later, Gélu called her the "instrument" through which the
marvelous liberation of Orléans had occurred. From that time he never
wavered in his support of her and recommended that the king consult
her in matters spiritual as well as temporal.

Furthermore, one of the greatest theologians of the time, Jean
Gerson, wrote a spirited defense of Joan when the king asked for his
reaction to the Poitiers examinations. Gerson's treatise was widely circulated in Europe in 1429, and it has survived. The Maid did not sub-
scribe to sorcery or witchcraft, Gerson wrote, and she sought no
advantage for herself—only for the honor of God and the survival of
France. Willing to risk personal danger to expel the English from
France, Joan was entirely justified in wearing male clothing and short

hair, he added: it was the only sensible style for her and only one of the elements indicating that her mission may be presumed to enjoy divine approval.*

JOAN'S OPENNESS TO God, in other words, had practical consequences that could be understood only with the passing of time—precisely the way every person discovers a meaning and purpose in life. In Joan's case fidelity to God's summons came to mean a commitment to alleviate human suffering by lifting the siege of Orléans. For now that was the essential meaning of "saving France"—not a political act but a humanitarian one. As for the crowning of Charles at Reims, it seems that this goal became clear only later, as a sort of coda after the successes at Orléans and elsewhere in the Loire Valley.

Saints are generally regarded as people who experienced a dramatic moment of illumination that forestalled any further doubt or darkness and forever sweetened pain or suffering. But this is a skewed vision of sainthood; it is also terribly wrongheaded spirituality. For one thing, it implies that God plays favorites—that some people are selected for a gift that warms and leavens all of life while the rest of us stumble along, deprived of some mechanism that could make life so much easier. But making life easier for oneself, like "feeling good about oneself," has nothing to do with authentic faith, nor is a relationship with God something about which one reaches final clarity. Holiness lies in a process of becoming more fully human.

In the Christian tradition, for example, the only model for faith is Jesus of Nazareth. His proclamation, one observes in the New Testament, was not particularly religious: he spoke of God, certainly, but

---

* Gerson's positive reaction to Joan was likely based only on her reputation and the report from Poitiers. It is unlikely that he knew of Joan's triumph at Orléans, for his treatise was concluded in Lyons on May 14, only six days after the siege was lifted.

only in relation to ordinary human life with its quotidian struggle and suffering. Nor did he speak or preach in especially religious or sectarian terms; in fact, it may be said that Jesus came to set the world free from enslavement to and obsession with mere (humanly made) religion. "He went about doing good" is the biblical summary of his life and mission, and no words are more moving or provocative.

In the life of Jesus we find no pattern of instant illumination and perfect understanding. To the contrary, he came only in stages to understand the contours of his mission to proclaim God's unfathomable and unimaginable love for all humankind and to reach out to people as healer and comforter. He entered adulthood as a disciple of John the Baptist; he then gathered a few followers when John was arrested and could preach no more; and finally he went out on his own only when John was executed, to take up where John had left off. It is certainly a misreading of the New Testament to say that everything was clear to Jesus from the start; to assert the contrary would be, for one thing, to deny the truth of his full humanity.

All of this is singularly important in any consideration of Joan of Arc. Gradually disclosed and discovered, her purpose and meaning were not specifically religious as we ordinarily use that word: they were not sectarian and did not use the props of religion. Hence for those who revere her as a saint, there has always been something slightly embarrassing and difficult to explain: her voices did not direct her into a convent or to found a hospital or a schoolroom; to the contrary, they sent her onto a battlefield. We need to recognize, however, that the battlefield was secondary: her mission was to alleviate the suffering of her compatriots, who were being starved out by the English. Only after mustering the troops and inspiring them to victory was she used in the coronation of Charles, which (as one scholar has written) "became part of her mission only in the course of the lengthy debates on strategy that took place between the princes of the blood and the king's military commanders in the aftermath of Orléans."

The interrogation of Joan at Poitiers concluded with another kind of examination. To confirm that Joan was no liar when she called herself *la Pucelle*, "the Maid," a group of women, under the supervision of the king's mother-in-law, was asked to confirm that Joan was indeed a virgin. The examination was performed; she was a virgin. Had the women determined otherwise, she would have been dismissed at once as a liar, and her entire claim and mission would have been rejected.

TWO DAYS BEFORE she left Poitiers to return to Chinon, Joan dictated a letter to be sent to the English commanders at Orléans. Dated Tuesday of Holy Week—March 22, 1429—the letter has survived:

> *To the King of England, and you, Duke of Bedford, who call yourself the regent of the kingdom of France; to William de la Pole, earl of Suffolk; to John, Lord Talbot; and to you, Thomas, Lord Scales, who call yourselves Bedford's lieutenants:*
>
> *Do right by the King of Heaven. Hand over to the king—who is sent here by God, the King of heaven—the keys to all the towns you have taken and plundered in France. The Maid is quite prepared to make peace, if you are willing to do right, so long as you give up France and make amends for occupying it.*
>
> *And you, archers, soldiers noble and otherwise, who are around the town of Orléans, in God's name, go back to your own lands. If you will not do so, beware: the Maid will come to see you very soon, to your great misfortune.... If you do not believe the tidings sent by God and the Maid, we will strike against you harshly, and we will see who will have the better right, God or you.*

By this time the report from Poitiers had reached Charles; however lacking in enthusiasm for Joan, the king's counselors saw that things had become so desperate for the Valois that the Maid could at least be given a chance to prove herself at Orléans. If she was even mildly successful, the fortunes of France just might improve; in any case, things could hardly be worse.

It is important to recall that the idea of a woman skilled in military matters was not unknown in the Middle Ages. As Joan's contemporary, Christine de Pisan, wrote in her *Book of the Three Virtues* (1406), it was expected that a noble Frenchwoman would know how to defend the family estate in her husband's absence:

> She should have a man's heart, which means that she should know the laws of warfare and all things pertaining to them, so that she will be prepared to command her men if there is need of it, knowing how to assault and defend, if the situation requires it.... She should try out her defenders and ascertain the quality of their courage and determination before putting too much trust in them, to see what strength and help she can count on in case of need; she should make sure of this and not put her trust in vain or feeble promises. She must give special attention to what resources she would have until her husband could get there.

On Thursday, March 24, Joan was back in Chinon. According to Simon Charles, master of the court of requests, the king gave her some troops, bestowed on her some military prerogatives, and gave her a place in the army. Her role became more important with each month, but it was not clearly specified in advance, nor was it the same every day of her campaigns. She encouraged the troops in a new and effective discipline and saw that their spiritual needs were met; she conferred with the military chieftains on strategy; and she led the men to victory in the most important battles. Joan's influence and activity were of surpassing importance, but she was neither the sole commander of operations nor a *chef de guerre*, unless we understand that the phrase was used imprecisely and could connote a flexible responsibility.

Because of Joan's enormous and historic influence, it would help to see precisely where she stood in the military hierarchy of Charles VII's reign. But such formal distinctions did not exist, and so she cannot be placed at a specific rank. Of course, the general commander of all forces was the king, but the practical supervisory task was assigned to the *connétable* or constable of France, who necessarily parceled out tasks to chieftains in various locations. In specific battles the officer was often chosen on the spot, on the basis of his wisdom, achievement, wealth, and influence (and, it was presumed, at least some military expertise). The command of the militia, in other words, was flexible and often improvised.

More clear was the hierarchy of the nobility. After the king came dukes, counts, viscounts, barons and lords (some of whom were not noblemen). By Joan's time the chivalric levels, mostly ordered by the Church, no longer had the symbolic role of earlier times. The chivalry, as it was called, consisted of knights, then squires (who aspired to be knights), and pages (who aspired to be squires).

Important at court were the so-called Grand Officers of the Crown—chamberlain, chancellor, constable, marshals, an admiral and the masters of crossbowmen and of the artillery. Perhaps most quaintly amusing to modern ears are the titles of those who worked in the royal household: the great wine waiter, the master baker, the master of the kitchen, the master of the horse, of the house, of the falcons, and finally the master of rivers and forests. Cupbearers, cellarers, and huntsmen were found in more or less profusion, depending on both season and need.

FROM APRIL 6 to 21, Joan was at Tours, where she was outfitted with a sword, armor, a new standard and a small staff or military household, which was typical for all captains; in her case the items and personnel provided her with both an honorary retinue and an added measure of security. Now she would be accompanied by a master of horse or squire, two pages, two heralds, and two chaplains.

At her trial Joan said that her voices had told her to send for an ancient and venerated sword, long buried at Saint-Catherine-de-Fierbois; messengers indeed found it, buried in an obscure location just as she had said. Contrary to pious legend, it is not necessary to see this as evidence of Joan's second sight or clairvoyance. The directions her voices provided to find the sword was perhaps Joan's way of recalling a sudden inspiration to have this particular one found and brought to her, since it came from a place with the hallowed connection to Saint Catherine. Joan had stopped at Fierbois, after all, and it is not unlikely that the story of the famous, mystical sword circulated among townspeople she met.

As for her full suit of armor, it was about sixty pounds of plates— a neckpiece of five or six overlapping sections, a kind of clasped steel blouson, plates covering the hips, a steel skirt and more steel pieces hinged for the elbows, knees, legs and feet. Her helmet most likely had a steel band at the chin and a visor that protected her face. Over all this was a woolen cloak. The royal treasury paid for the armor as well as for that supplied to her brothers Pierre and Jean, who had come to join her militia.* Joan's new standard, painted by a Scots mercenary, was made of white satin, with an image of a dove holding the legend *De par le Roy du Ciel*, "On behalf of the King of Heaven." In addition she had a larger personal standard or pennon: Christ flanked by angels and surrounded by gold fleur-de-lis and the names of Jesus and Mary. The standard and pennon were not merely decorative but practical: because she would be completely enclosed in armor, a distinguishing sign was required, both to rally the troops and to identify her whereabouts.

---

* Apart from their presence among her troops, no details have survived about Joan's brothers, who survived her.

Joan's household was formed quickly. Jean d'Aulon was sent from the dauphin's service at Chinon to serve as her squire, or master of horse; he did so until her capture the following year. Her two pages were Louis de Coutes and another teenager named Raymond, who was Joan's standard-bearer. These young men aspired to knighthood and served variously as servants-at-arms and general assistants.

Joan was honored with not one (as usual) but two pursuivants, or apprentice heralds, named Ambleville and Guyenne. Heralds were messengers, and as such they had a kind of immunity, for the chivalric code strictly forbade killing the messenger. Only high-ranking nobles had full-status heralds; Joan's were almost certainly pursuivants.

Jean Pasquerel, an Augustinian monk, was Joan's primary chaplain. He had apparently met her parents on a pilgrimage and was introduced to Joan through them, after they had received her letter of apology and been reconciled to their daughter. "Joan's parents had come [to Tours] to see her," Pasquerel recalled, "and they knew me and brought me to her, saying, 'Joan, we have brought you this good Father; if you knew him well, you would love him very much.'" He remained with her as confessor and spiritual director from that day until her capture the following year.

At Tours the chaplain saw that Joan was growing more anxious each day. "She had not been pleased with all the interrogations, which had prevented her from accomplishing the work for which she was sent. She said that the need and the right time to act had arrived." At Joan's request, Pasquerel had a banner made with an image of the crucifixion; this was carried by a procession of clergy on the march to Orléans. The second chaplain was Nicolas de Vouthon, a relative of her mother; a third cleric, Mathelin Rouel, had no spiritual duties but kept the household accounts.

On April 21 Joan and her retinue set out for Blois, about thirty miles northeast of Tours and halfway to Orléans. There food supplies were loaded into caravans and the troops were assembled to meet her and to make plans for the journey and the onslaught against the enemy siege. Of the thousand warriors, half were men-at-arms and the rest bowmen.

"That company of men had great confidence in her," Louis de Coutes recalled. "She continually exhorted the soldiers to trust God completely." His impression was supported by her soldiers: "In the conduct and disposition of the army," according to Thiband d'Armagnac, whose assessment was typical, "and in the matter of warfare, in drawing up the order of troops in battle, and in the task of encouraging the men, Joan acted like an experienced, shrewd captain—as if all her life had been spent learning about war." To her great pleasure, Joan found the men quite ready to be inspired by the possibility of liberating Orléans and by her conviction that it could and would indeed be accomplished, but only by God's help.

The necessary artillery had also arrived—crossbows, longbows, lances, swords, maces and cannons. Longbowmen could dispatch up to eight arrows in one minute. Crossbowmen had a mechanical weapon that reached from great distances. Foot soldiers carried lethal poleaxes. Halberders were named for their halberd, an ax blade topped by a thick spike that could decapitate or sever limbs with a single blow. Other warriors carried light but deadly scythes. And handgunners were equipped with culverins, which predated rifles; they were among the first weapons to benefit from the invention of gunpowder. On the ground rather than on horseback, ramparts or ladders, the *coutillers* carried a broad, double-edged blade for their grisly task: to cut the throats of wounded men who could not pay a ransom and so could not be taken prisoner. As Joan would see to her horror, war was a dreadful and dehumanizing enterprise.

At Blois she was joined by important men loyal to the king, of whom two deserve an introduction. Étienne de Vignolles had also come from Orléans to meet the Maid and to return with the troops under her leadership. A crude man with a short temper, he loved battle but had no taste for culture; he was, however, faithful and true to Joan's leadership. Vignolles was given the nickname La Hire, which was perhaps related to the Latin *ira*, meaning "anger"; experienced in the military, he was renowned for his salty language and an irrepressible inclination toward banditry, which were suppressed during his expeditions with Joan. Rough though he was, La Hire became one of her most trusted allies. His prayer, remarkable in its bold confidence, has survived: "O God, please do for La Hire what you would like La Hire to do for you—if you were La Hire and La Hire were God."

And then there was Gilles de Laval, the wealthy twenty-five-year-old Baron de Rais. He accompanied Joan as one of her most ardent and loyal supporters from Blois to Paris and distinguished himself on and off the battlefield. But a few years after he left her company, something went very wrong. He squandered one of the most enormous fortunes in France and then turned to a life of appalling degeneracy: de Rais and several henchmen have the doubtful distinction of being named among the world's first serial killers. They captured, raped, and tortured to death about two hundred boys between the ages of six and eighteen, and finally, after lengthy and difficult trials, Gilles de Rais was executed at the age of thirty-six. But in 1429 none of this could have been imagined as the future of this learned and sophisticated soldier, so reliable was he in his duties and service to Joan.

Also in her caravan were Jean de Metz and Bertrand de Poulengy, the first acting as treasurer for the group, the second as a squire.

THE MAID'S FIRST order of business during their meetings at Blois had to do with soldiers' conduct. She encouraged her men to receive the Eucharist from their chaplains and to refrain from foul language and any inappropriate use of holy names. Jean d'Aulon kept clear memories of the profoundly religious atmosphere Joan created: "Twice a day, morning and evening, she assembled the priests, with whom she sang anthems and hymns, and she invited the soldiers to go to one of them for private confession. When we were on the march to Orléans, we were led by our clergy with the banner [of the crucifixion]."

Centuries later, it is often presumed that such a pious tone and environment would create boredom, cynicism, and even open rebellion among any militia. But in an era when faith was a fact of life, prayer was ubiquitous, ritual respected, and the presence of clergymen taken seriously, the result was a fresh discipline and respect—even a chivalric courtliness—among many of the troops. Joan herself was so obviously and sincerely devout that the major captains of her men-at-arms and crossbowmen were more than impressed: they followed her example as best they could.

But the Maid did issue an order that many among her troops may have resented. "She would not have any women accompany the army," recalled Louis de Coutes, speaking of Joan's intolerance of camp prostitutes. "Once, near the town of Château-Thierry, she saw the mistress of one of the soldiers. The Maid pursued the woman ... and warned her gently and charitably that she must be no longer found in the company of the soldiers." Alençon and the squire Simon Beaucroix testified similarly: "She detested the women who follow soldiers," related the former. "She would never have women of evil life in the army with the soldiers," according to the latter. "When she found any of them, she obliged them to go away—unless the soldiers were willing to take them as wives."

Joan's injunction against camp prostitutes was more than moral outrage: it was a way of establishing discipline among her soldiers, whose lassitude for war—based on their failing fortunes—had led them easily to the usual pastimes: gambling, excessive drinking, and (as the English called it) whoring. But her prohibition of camp followers was also an emblem of her conviction that women ought not to be merely used. She herself was a natural leader, and a situation of women in sexual-economic exploitation was naturally repellent to her.

The fact is that before her arrival, the ambition and spirit of the French military depended on class associations, fraternal organizations, and political-financial alliances. As one scholar of the war has written, however, "[Joan's] imposition of sterner morals on these armies largely seems to have been accepted by the common soldiers. She demanded a great deal, [and] the result was a startling increase in French morale which was soon reinforced by military success."

And what of Joan's presence among so many young, armed men? Perhaps of all the nobles and military men, the Duke of Alençon—that dedicated, courageous and skillful commander—may be trusted most. Although he was a man who had a keen eye for attractive and available women, he too recognized a rare quality of sincere devotion that deflected any tendency to make sexual overtures. "Sometimes I lay down to sleep with Joan and the soldiers," Alençon recalled. "We were all in the straw together, and sometimes I saw Joan prepare for the night. Sometimes too I looked at her breasts, which were beautiful. And yet I never had any carnal desire for her."

Gobert Thibault, a royal squire, confirmed the soldiers' uncommon reaction to so appealing a young woman. "I heard many of those closest to her say that they sometimes felt a carnal urge for her, but they never dared to act on it. Often when they were speaking among themselves about fornication and saying things that might arouse desire, they were not able to continue such talk if they saw her or if she came near. I questioned several of those who sometimes slept the night in Joan's company, and they answered as I have." These recollections do not contradict the testimonies that earlier Joan had slept fully dressed on the way from Vaucouleurs to Chinon; she was now wearing heavy armor, which had to be removed at night.

On April 27, in a long procession headed by priests carrying the crucifixion banner and leading them in singing hymns, Joan and the men left Blois and headed toward Orléans. Up to this time some important and influential military leaders had firmly avoided support of any effort to liberate Orléans, but now the general attitude had shifted in favor of Charles and the Maid.

FIVE

The New Deborah

(April–June 1429)

O ne of the most appealing cities of France, Orléans lies on the north bank of the Loire, sixty miles south of Paris. By 1429 it had been capital of a duchy for over a century and was fortified by ramparts, with towers at regular intervals. Ordinarily protected by its resident duke, Orléans suffered a profound loss of morale when he was imprisoned in England; the defense of the city was then undertaken by his half-brother, Jean, Count of Dunois.

The ramparts of the walled city were strategically maintained, as were the city's five gates: the Burgundy gate, through which ran the road southeast to Gien; the Paris gate, only for pedestrians at the time of the siege; the Bernier gate, with its road north to Paris; the Renard gate, through which travelers proceeded southwest toward Blois; and the Saint Catherine gate, on the harbor, which connected to the bridge and to the south or left bank of the Loire. Each gate had two towers connected by a drawbridge.

DURING THE SUMMER of 1428 the English had sailed from Southampton to Harfleur in Normandy. From there they marched to Paris and onward to Chartres. Establishing footholds west and south of Orléans, the invaders—in a four-week period from early September to October—took the nearby towns of Meung, Beaugency, and Jargeau. Now began the formation of siege positions around Orléans.

That winter the forces of Dunois and of La Hire tried unsuccessfully to break the stranglehold around Orléans and to prevent the English advance toward the dauphin while other French troops attempted to intercept a major English supply caravan near Rouvray. These maneuvers failed miserably, and most of the king's men retreated south to Tours, Chinon and Bourges. By the spring of 1429 French morale could not have been lower.

As one noted historian has rightly observed about the months leading up to the liberation of Orléans, "To describe this series of events in terms of a strategic plan is probably wrong. What the French commanders did with brilliant success was to take prompt advantage of rapidly changing circumstances. In doing so, they showed themselves to be military leaders of the finest quality." As for Joan, she "ensured that the French assaults maintained their momentum despite heavy casualties. What was, however, new was the degree of French commitment to the capture of such siege-works in the face of the large number of guns which they contained."

That commitment would not have been effective without Joan, who was regarded as a daughter of God—a girl blessed with a mystical gift of insight and faith. To understand her value to the military expeditions, it is essential to appreciate the strength of religious belief at that time and the veneration in which people held an evidently prayerful woman vowed to virginity.

Later, Napoleon could have been referring to Joan of Arc when he insisted that sustaining morale was the most critical aspect of successful combat. An effective standard-bearer, she knew when boldness was indicated. Her daring was not always justified, but because of her the French troops acted more bravely than ever. The *chefs de guerre* for this expedition were military men and others appointed directly by Charles, but because of the loyalty Joan evoked from the troops, their leaders had to consider her advice and often comply with it.

This complex of ideas was demonstrated when the company left Blois on April 27. Joan, the supply caravan, and troops assigned to her were escorted northeastward, proceeding south of the Loire and thus avoiding the English-held towns. The fact that she was led along but did not determine the route indicates that she was not in command of these soldiers: they were "hers" only insofar as she was their moral support, their spiritual patron and champion and sometimes even a source of counsel in military strategy.

On Friday, April 29, Joan was furious when she realized that she and her convoy had been led to bypass Orléans and that there would be a delay in the assault against the English. She was met on the banks of the Loire by Dunois, called the Bastard of Orléans, which implied neither shame nor social stigma. He was the natural son of the former Duke of Orléans but was born out of wedlock, a situation without any attachment of disgrace. At the time illegitimate children were openly acknowledged by their fathers and received all the prerogatives, titles, and inheritances of legitimate offspring.

Dunois soon became a staunch ally and a good friend to Joan, but things started badly between them. Confronting Dunois on the south bank of the Loire, Joan made no attempt to hide her anger. "Are you the Bastard of Orléans?"

"I am indeed, and I rejoice at your arrival."

"Are you the one who gave the order that I come here, on this side of the river, so that I could not go directly to [engage and attack] the English?"

Dunois replied that this had been the best and safest counsel of his and the king's advisers.

"In God's name," Joan shouted, "the counsel of our Lord God is wiser and safer than yours. You thought you could trick me, and instead you trick yourself. I am here with better help than any soldier ever brought to any city—the help of the King of Heaven."

Dunois may have been offended by her impatience and impudence, but there was no time to argue about courtly manners or expeditious travel routes. They were awaiting the arrival of supply boats, which were to ferry men and goods across the river to Orléans prior to the main assault. This fleet had come upriver from Blois and was now sailing against the tide, the wind, and the current, making the passage both late and perilous. But suddenly—while Joan was sparring with Dunois—the situation changed. The wind direction shifted, the water level rose, and the company was easily transported across the river with the supply boats. The troops regarded this propitious turn of events as miraculous, a sure sign of divine guidance because of Joan's presence, and so her credibility advanced along with French determination. "From that moment," Dunois said, "I had good hope in her—more than ever before."

To skeptics it seems downright gullible to interpret as miraculous a favorable turning of tide, which is quite a natural event. The Israelites of ancient history reacted similarly when they were fleeing Egyptian oppression and came to the sea: an auspicious shift in tide and wind enabled them to traverse a normally flooded isthmus, and by the time the pursuing enemy arrived, the waters had returned. But the event was seen, then and later, through the lens of faith: God had acted on behalf of His people through the ordinary patterns of nature. The wonderful aspect was the timing.

In the Middle Ages there was no sense that some things were "natural" and some were "supernatural." The world belonged to God, and He managed things to suit His purpose. Faith confirmed that God is always present and active, working in and through His world, however mysteriously and often incomprehensibly. It was no different for the French, who readily regarded their passage across the river as divinely guided. There was no room in their thinking for mere coincidence or accident. The universe and God's activity in it were considered too mysterious to be predicted or comprehended.

This apparently small event—large to her countrymen—was but one example of what Joan offered her troops: no worldly compensation but a pointer toward something like a religious vocation. This primary motivation and spiritual atmosphere did not, of course, make things easier for the soldiers; faith is not an anesthetic. Nor did they become saints. They still felt mortal terror, they tried to avoid injury, and they became fiercely angry at the enemy and aimed lethal blows. Was there a difference, then, between the French under Joan and the English under their commanders? There was indeed, and it had to do with the grander purpose of their battle: to save France, which was sacred to them and, they believed, to God.

What Joan impressed on the men by her faith and her actions, then, had more to do with the things of God than the machinery of war or prevailing politics. For her the struggle against English occupation and the eventual permanent establishment of French sovereignty were matters of justice, and justice was regarded as a major virtue in the Middle Ages. From justice came the origins of chivalry, which was about much more than mere courtesy: it concerned the order of a sovereign society and its place in the economy of God's plan for the world.

RELATIVE TO HER sense of justice was Joan's repeated reminder to her soldiers that whether they lived or died, their efforts would win them eternal life—their proper reward. This was not presumptuous: it sprang from a confidence that God would not reject those who fought bravely for a just cause. With the threat of danger haunting every step of every day, with the possibility of wounds or the loss of limbs on a battlefield, with the chance of capture and foreign imprisonment, troops had to be constantly encouraged. Can it be said then that hers was a mission of faith? And if it was, precisely how did she manage to inspire faith and to attract loyalty from thousands of men of varying temperaments, characters, attitudes, values, and backgrounds?

Joan saw justice and the sovereignty of France as indissolubly linked. The result of securing France's freedom from English imperialism was to be justice in the land, the exclusion of aggressors, and finally peace. In the fifteenth century the only means of securing the first step—legitimate rule—was by and in battle; she simply had no other method available to her. Negotiators could not be summoned with all dispatch; there were no swift means of communication, nor were there safe territories for men to sit down and work out a treaty; and both sides were scattered in disarray. But by letter and in person, she begged the English to depart peacefully before the French took up arms to liberate Orléans.

Despite the fact that Joan of Arc is most often portrayed with armor and sword, the truth is that she hated bloodshed and longed for peace. She refused to wield her own sword in battle: it was used as a threat to the enemy and, held aloft, as a signal to her soldiers. For her, war was not an exciting, enlivened game of chess. It was real, earnest and dreadful. But it was also a tragic necessity if France were to survive.

On the question of Joan's faith and her attraction of others' loyalty, it is a matter of record that she evoked a greater and deeper commitment from her troops than did any other commander of her time, and they kept alive their memories of her and her abilities. Joan was for her contemporaries as she has been for six centuries after her death: someone who could not be reduced to a footnote in history.

Why did the king, nobles, royal counselors and so many ordinary Frenchmen respond to her challenge? First, it is critical to remember that the fifteenth century was a time in which many forms of popular piety flourished—most significantly, devotion to women saints, those who were long or recently deceased. But many living women were also regarded as saints: this was the idea of the mulieres sanctae, or living holy women, to whom respect and veneration were due. That notion may be clearly seen in the respect Joan received from Jean de Metz, Bertrand de Poulengy, Jean d'Alençon, and other men to whom she was often physically proximate and who at first responded understandably to her appeal but never made a sexual advance.

As the king's squire, Gobert Thibault, observed, "Everyone followed her." The contemporary *Journal of the Siege of Orléans* added, "All regarded her with much affection—men and women, as well as small children. There was an extraordinary rush to touch her, or even to touch the horse on which she sat." This occurred only because (as one contemporary scholar has noted), "she brought action and victory, while older, noble generals had achieved nothing but inaction and defeat."

Joan was not the only woman in history to inspire and to give directions to soldiers. The Greek poet Telesilla was famous for saving the city of Argos from attack by Spartan troops in the fifth century B.C. In first-century Britain, Queen Boudicca led an uprising against the occupying Roman forces. In the third century Zenobia, Queen of Palmyra (latter-day Syria), declared her independence of the Roman Empire and seized Egypt and much of Asia Minor. Africa had its rebel Queen Gwedit, or Yodit, in the tenth century. In the eleventh appeared Sikelgaita, a Lombard princess who frequently accompanied her husband, Robert, on his Byzantine military campaigns, in which she fought in full armor, rallying Robert's troops when they were initially repulsed by the Byzantine army. In the twelfth century Eleanor of Aquitaine took part in the Second Crusade, and in the fourteenth century Joanna, Countess of Montfort, took up arms after her husband died in order to protect the rights of her son, the Duke of Brittany. She organized resistance and, dressed in full armor, led a raid of knights that successfully destroyed one of the enemy's rear camps.

Joan was not a queen, a princess, a noblewoman or a respected poet with public support. She went to her task at enormous physical risk to both her virginity and her life, and at considerable risk of a loss of both reputation and influence. The English, for example, constantly referred to her as a prostitute: to them, she must have been; otherwise, why would she travel with an army of men?

Yet Joan was undeterred by peril or slander, precisely because of her confidence that God was their captain and leader. She often said that if she had been unsure of that, she would not have risked such obvious danger but would have kept to her simple, rural life in Domrémy.

AT EIGHT O'CLOCK on the evening of Friday, April 29, Joan entered Orléans with Dunois, La Hire, de Rais, her personal staff, her brothers, various captains and about two hundred men-at-arms. Because the English did not have enough men to surround the city completely and had left the east gate undefended, the French arrived unmolested.

The population of the city was just under twenty thousand, and most of the citizens came out to meet them with torches, "rejoicing as if God Himself had come among them—and not without reason, for they had endured much difficulty, and were afraid of not being rescued, of losing their goods and perhaps their lives" if they resisted the English occupiers. Thus reported the contemporary *Journal of the Siege of Orléans*, which added colorful details by eyewitnesses:

> The townspeople already felt comforted by the virtue of that simple Maid, whom they regarded with strong affection. There was a huge crowd, with everyone trying to touch her or her horse. One of the men bearing torches came so close to her that her standard caught fire. But she put it out calmly. "My Lord has sent me to help this good town of Orléans," she told the crowd. "Hope in God—and if you do, you shall be delivered from your enemies."

Joan and her retinue were taken for a night's lodging to the house of Jacques Boucher, the town treasurer. The English troops, meantime, were occupied with constructing new blockades and shifting many of their forces to points south of the river.

On Saturday, April 30, the troops of Dunois confronted the English at their crucial defense point, a strategy apparently undertaken to distract them while the last of the supplies were brought into the city. At the same time Joan hurried toward Les Tourelles, the fortified towers guarding the approach to the city on a bridge over the river. She had had enough of interrogations and examinations, plans and preparations. Now she wanted action.

Whoever held Les Tourelles essentially held Orléans, and in this case it was Sir William Glasdale, in command of English troops. With her usual audacity, Joan ordered him to abandon the siege, a demand that was countered by Glasdale's insults. He would never surrender to a prostitute like Joan, he shouted down to her; furthermore, if he could capture her he would immediately burn her at the stake.

The next few days were eerily quiet. On Sunday, May 1, Dunois and La Hire borrowed money from the citizens of Orléans to pay the soldiers; a few hours later Dunois departed for Blois, planning to return soon with cash and more troops. Meanwhile, people nearly battered down the door of the Boucher house to see Joan, to touch her garments, to offer food and supplies. She and her companions then rode through the streets of the city, encouraging everyone just as she did the soldiers. God would not abandon them, she said over and over: He held them and the cause of France in His hands. She also studied the geography of the town, considering the places most advantageous for defense. The next day they ventured outside the city walls, where Joan made a careful assessment of the English preparations for battle: they were not, she considered, as daunting as some of the French captains had predicted.

On Wednesday, May 4, La Hire went out to secure the safe reentry of Dunois, who returned from Blois with reinforcements. The precise sequence of events that day is obscure, but at some point—quite

on her own and without informing Dunois or La Hire—Joan rode
out to join about fifteen hundred men in an assault on English
attackers; according to the *Journal of the Siege of Orléans*, the mere
sight of her brought cheers from the French soldiers. Enguerrand
de Monstrelet, who was partial to the Burgundian cause and therefore antagonistic to Joan, wrote an accurate picture of this day in
his contemporary *Chronicles*:

> After rising early, Joan spoke to several captains and soldiers, per-
> suading them to arm and follow her because she wanted, as she
> put it, to get at the enemy, adding that she knew they would be
> defeated. They were amazed at what she said, but they neverthe-
> less armed and went with her to that part of the English fortifica-
> tions known as the Bastille Saint-Loup, which was particularly
> strong. It was held by three or four hundred English, but they
> were soon beaten and all of them either killed, wounded or cap-
> tured, and the tower [was] demolished and burned. Then the
> Maid returned to Orléans with all the knights and men she had
> led, and there she was joyfully acclaimed by all ranks of men.

Other sources add that one hundred Englishmen were killed, a
slaughter that brought Joan to tears, and forty were taken prisoner. In
light of this victory the French felt even more confident—and their loyalty to the Maid was all the greater.

The Feast of the Ascension was celebrated on Thursday the fifth,
and there were no military excursions or calls to arms. But strategic
choices had to be made, and Dunois called a war council that included
La Hire, Raoul de Gaucourt, Gilles de Rais and, for the first time, Joan.
Should the French attack the weakened English positions on the north
bank of the Loire or launch an onslaught on Les Tourelles? The latter
was chosen, dangerous though they knew it was. As for the tactics to
be used, Dunois and Joan were strongly at odds; Gaucourt supported

Dunois, but most of the others (and the ordinary men-at-arms) agreed with Joan's plans. At the same time, messengers arrived with word that a large English platoon was coming down from Paris. That afternoon Joan dictated another letter to the English; in addition to being a plea for peace, it also exemplified her sense of humor. The message was delivered by a crossbowman who shot it into Les Tourelles:

> You men of England, who have no right to this kingdom of France, the King of Heaven orders and notifies you through me, Joan the Maid, to leave your fortresses and go back to your own country—or I will produce a clash of arms to be eternally remembered. This is the third and last time I have written to you, and I shall not write anything further.[*] I would have sent this letter in a more proper form, but you have arrested my heralds. Please send them back to me, and I will send some of your men, captured in the fortress, for they are not all dead.

The English response was another flurry of insults. On Friday, May 6, the simmering drama became an open crisis. Joan led the men directly toward Les Tourelles, Dunois and the others following her despite their preference for a roundabout route. Near their destination Joan and her companions realized that they were no longer numerous enough to withstand the English from so vulnerable a position below the towers. The *Journal of the Siege of Orléans* documented what next occurred: "The English rushed out of the Tourelles in great numbers, shouting and charging violently. But despite their disadvantage, Joan and La Hire and all their army attacked the English with such great force and courage that they [the English] were forced to retreat back to the towers."

---

[*] The first warning was contained in the letter of March 22; a letter similar to that of May 5 had already been sent on April 30.

Dunois and his cohorts wanted the soldiers to have a rest after this excursion, but Joan would not hear of it, and the men rose up to agree with her. Now that they seemed to have an advantage, they wanted to attack in full force the next morning to take Les Tourelles, especially because it was obvious that the English did not move any additional troops to that strategic place. As for the people of Orléans, they were by now virtually unanimous in support of Joan's decisions and advice; to show their approval of her plans, according to the *Journal*, "they labored through the night to bring food, bread, and wine to the men-at-arms who were in the vanguard."

On Saturday morning, May 7, Joan and her troops were ready to go. When they reached the gate of the city, however, they were stopped by Raoul de Gaucourt, Dunois's second in command. Told not to proceed, Joan replied coolly, "Like it or not, the soldiers will go forth, and they will prevail as they always have." So, she added, he ought not to act like an obstacle, a bad man. Gaucourt yielded.

Les Tourelles were defended by about eight hundred Englishmen; Joan went forth with perhaps half that number of French soldiers. Surrounding the towers, they were bombarded with arrows, axes, spears, spiked clubs and even cannonballs when they tried to climb up, and the conflict quickly turned into the most violent and deadly clash since the battle of Agincourt. Undaunted and shouting both prayers and imprecations against the enemy, the French continued bravely, placing ladders against the towers and rapidly scaling them, demonstrating remarkable perseverance even as their comrades were cut down all around them.

Suddenly, as she was planting a ladder against the fort at the bridge, an Englishman's arrow was aimed toward Joan at an angle, hitting its mark perfectly, piercing a seam in her plate armor and searing through the flesh between her neck and shoulder to a depth of several inches. For a few moments she tried to ignore the wound and the protruding arrow, which could not easily be torn out. But then the pain became too severe, and when her squires saw her pale features, they carried her away from the center of action.

Her friends assessed the injury, which was not life threatening but could become so if she lost a quantity of blood or succumbed to infection. By this time Joan was shaking with fear and probably with a fever, and the pain made her cry out in great sobs. A few plates of armor were then removed and the arrow quickly wrenched out, fortunately, with the deadly tip intact. Available swatches of cloth were used to stop the flow of blood, but nothing alleviated Joan's pain. Olive oil was applied as an antiseptic and analgesic, and a soldier asked if she wished them to pronounce a popular magical incantation. She welcomed the oil but forbade anything to do with superstition. Hours later she was back in the battle.

By early evening the French had no advantage over their enemy, and Dunois suggested retreating to the city until the next day. Joan would hear nothing of it; instead she took up her standard and stuck it in a prominent ditch near the action. At once the English were so astonished they thought she might indeed be someone with supernatural powers. At the same time, the French were heartened at the sight of her. "They regained their courage," Dunois recalled, "and began to climb up again … so that, at about eight o'clock that evening, many Englishmen were in flight."

There was one last sortie: enemy forces tried to make a surprise return to Les Tourelles to recover their advantage, but the drawbridge collapsed under pressure from a boat, deliberately set afire and launched in the direction of the bridge. "Few among them could escape," Jean d'Aulon recalled, "for the four or five hundred soldiers they numbered were all killed or drowned." Weighed down by their armor, most of the English, including their commander, Sir William Glasdale, could not swim, and others were unable to draw them out of the Loire. Seeing this, the few remaining comrades in the towers surrendered and most of the army withdrew toward the towns of Meung and Jargeau, which they still held.

Several witnesses attested that Joan wept openly at the sight of so many deaths. Urging the surviving Englishmen to avoid a similar death, she told them to leave at once on their own lest a worse fate befall them. Her remark was later misinterpreted as a threat that she would put some curse or other on them—and this supported the idea that Joan was a witch with demonic powers. Still weeping at the carnage on both sides, she was then taken to her lodging, where a doctor was summoned to care for her injury.

The next morning, Sunday, May 8, the English gathered in battle array between their siege lines and the walls of Orléans. This was either a gesture of insolent bravado or an attempt to prevent the French from attacking them as they withdrew. Or perhaps they hoped the French would indeed attack; most likely the lineup reflected a complex of all three motives. And so, outside the walls, the French faced the English, horses opposite horses and riders staring down riders. Joan and the other commanders ordered their forces not to attack. For an hour the scene was uncannily suspenseful. Then the English quietly turned and departed. The French kept their ground, savoring their victory as they watched the last of the enemy disappear over the horizon.

Joan and company returned to Orléans, where there was general rejoicing: the cathedral bells tolled, and a thanksgiving procession wound through the streets and alleys of the city. The siege had lasted two hundred ten days, and in only nine it had been lifted. "The people expressed joy in every way," according to the *Journal of the Siege of Orléans*, "giving wondrous praise to their valiant defenders, but most of all to the Maid." The occasion, in fact, marked the turning point of the Hundred Years' War: British hegemony in France had been broken, and the survival of France was no longer a dim hope but a distinct probability.

◆   ◆   ◆

MESSENGERS RODE AT once to the king at Chinon, bearing news that confirmed what Joan had promised: she had been sent by God to help save France, and God had not failed them. "Dear and well-beloved subjects," Charles wrote to the cities still supporting him, "we know that nothing will bring you greater joy than to hear the good news ..." and he detailed the battle, the situation of the walled city, the courage of the French, and the taking of Les Tourelles. "We exhort you to honor the virtuous acts and wondrous things reported to us, and also the Maid, who was present in person at the achievement of all these deeds."

The news was also heard in Paris, still held by the Burgundians on behalf of the English. Clément de Fauquembergue, clerk of the *parlement*, made a note of what the messengers had relayed: "On Tuesday, the tenth day of May, it was reported and circulated in Paris that on the previous Sunday, after repeated battles, a significant number of French troops ... entered Orléans and attacked the bridge of the city ... [and] in their company was a maid, who held her banner between the two enemy forces."

It has been customary since the early twentieth century to devalue, even dismiss, Joan's exploits and real accomplishments during the short span of her activity. Her detractors, with frank condescension, praise her religious sincerity but not her ability to muster the troops. Frenchmen like Anatole France reckoned that Joan was a victim of hallucinations, but he patted her as if she were an adorable mascot, refusing to attribute to her anything more significant than spiritual fervor. This belittlement perhaps tells us not so much about the facts of history as it does about the cynicism of writers who are unable to credit a woman whose deeds altered the course of history.

The testimony of Joan's contemporaries, however, is very different from the suppositions of modern cynics. Dunois felt that her activities were so remarkable "that even two or three of the most seasoned captains would not have made so good a plan," and Alençon confirmed that "everyone was astonished that she acted with the wisdom and perception of men with twenty or thirty years of experience." Some of the "wisdom" may in fact be traced to the peasant background derided by so many sophisticates.

Joan was persistently pragmatic: her goals were specific, realistic and congruent with her faith and morals. Critics to the contrary notwithstanding, she did not leave all military decisions to the men, nor (after they were in the thick of Orléans) was she excluded from councils of war. She made the decision to attack Les Tourelles, and she would not retreat from this assault despite her wound. Jean Luillier, a citizen of Orléans, put the matter simply when he said that he "and all the people of the city believed that if the Maid had not come from God to help them, all the inhabitants and the city itself would have quickly succumbed to the power of the enemy besieging them."

It was not her military expertise that won her the enduring loyalty of her people; it was rather Joan's utter and complete fidelity toward God that evoked reverence. Thus little time passed before poets and chroniclers compared her to Deborah, Esther and Judith, formidable women in the Hebrew Scriptures who heeded messages from God and brought relief to their people at critical times. Deborah victoriously led a coalition of tribal militias against a Canaanite army. Another threat to the Hebrew people was put down through the intervention of Esther, and Judith was a faithful widow who captivated and then decapitated the Assyrian general Holofernes. Joan did not share the bloodlust of these ancient heroines, but she was regarded as in their tradition, equally patriotic and just as effective on behalf of her nation. As early as that summer, the Hebrew heroines appear in a famous poem about the Maid by Christine de Pisan, written and circulated in July 1429.

It was, then, Joan's victories that impressed others. She insisted on having a chaplain among her retinue to celebrate Mass daily for her and to attend to the spiritual lives of her soldiers, and she deplored the inevitable suffering endured by both the French and English. Perhaps it is an unacceptable aspect of the story for later times: Joan's compatriots welcomed and revered the holiness she brought into their midst. She never said that anything was miraculous; much less did she claim to be unique or singularly gifted. Rather, she had a specific vocation, and she would be true to it. She listened, she believed, she obeyed.

SIX

"I Won't Fly Away!"

(May–July 1429)

Weakened by her wound but eager to proceed with her mission, Joan did not remain at Orléans to accept the tributes and gifts prepared by a grateful public. Instead, on Monday, May 9, she left the city with Dunois, La Hire, Gilles de Rais and her personal retinue. Their destination was Loches, ninety miles south, where the king was in residence at another royal castle; they arrived on May 11.

The group had not come to be honored or thanked; they wanted troops in order to liberate the Loire Valley from English hands—specifically, the towns of Meung, Jargeau and Beaugency—and thus to provide a safe route for the king to travel to Reims for his anointing, which had obviously been a matter of discussion among Joan and her companions. Here we see one of the first indications of the second part of Joan's campaign. Later Dunois testified that he went with her "to the king, at Loches, to ask him to give them men-at-arms so they could take Meung, Beaugency and Jargeau, which would permit them to go more freely and safely to Reims for the consecration."

She had no doubt about the next stage of the conflict or about the necessity of an expeditious coronation, and she advised the king not to hesitate. But his councilors were not so sure, and Charles first considered trying to take back Normandy. One of his advisers, Christophe d'Harcourt, asked Joan to speak openly about what her divine counsel advised, and that request was repeated by Charles himself: "Joan, won't you please tell us what he [Harcourt] asks, here, in the presence of my court?"

According to the testimony of Dunois, who was present, Joan said that whenever people asked about her spiritual counsel, she withdrew for prayer, during which she heard a voice: "Daughter of God, go, go, go, for I will be there to help. Go."

That faith, and Joan's natural importunity, carried the day. In light of the triumph at Orléans, Charles said, they would go to Reims. From Loches Joan proceeded to Saint-Florent-lès-Saumur, where she rested at the home of Alençon and his family. He was to be the commander, as Dunois had been at Orléans, and Joan outlined her plan for the recapture of the Loire Valley. Alençon's young wife was anxious for his safety. "Don't worry," Joan assured her. "I'll bring him back safe and sound—and maybe even better than he is now!"

By early June they were on their way, separating occasionally to recruit volunteers in various villages. Two young brothers joined them, Guy and André de Laval (cousin of Gilles de Laval, the baron de Rais). On June 8 Guy wrote to their mother about Joan's visit to them in Selles:

On Monday [June 6], I went to see the Maid. She had some wine brought in and said, "Next time, we'll all drink it in Paris!" Seeing and hearing her, and observing her manner and actions, everything about her seemed to me a blessing from God [sont choses toutes divines]. She left in the evening for Romorantin, wearing white [that is, polished] armor and accompanied by men-at-arms. She rode a black horse . . . a page held her standard, and one of her brothers departed with her. . . . This morning the Duke of Alençon arrived with a great retinue. I played a game of handball with

him—and won. He is leaving this evening with Dunois and
Gaucourt to follow the Maid....

Alençon was entirely content to take seriously Joan's advice about
upcoming strategy, and with an army of about two thousand men the
Loire Valley campaign was successful—despite her disagreements with
some captains about whether Jargeau or Beaugency ought to be
attacked first. According to Alençon, Joan said that the former town
ought definitely to be their primary goal; she was "certain that God was
leading their cause—and if she did not believe that, she would have
preferred to be home taking care of her father's sheep and avoiding all
this danger." At first the lightly armed men of the expedition attacked
Jargeau without help, but they were repulsed by the English. Then
Joan, carrying her banner and leading the knights and more heavily
armored men, joined with reinforcements (mostly cannons, collected
after the English abandoned Orléans).

The victory at Jargeau was achieved on Sunday, June 12, but not
without some suspenseful moments: Joan's good friend Alençon, for
example, narrowly escaped lethal injury. Three hundred English and
Burgundian troops died, and as many French; as always, Joan took no
pleasure in the enemy's casualties. She was near a young English soldier who had been severely wounded and was lying on the ground,
bleeding profusely and moaning. At that moment one of her troops
approached and began to beat the injured boy with a club. Joan rode
up, angrily dismissed the Frenchman, and tenderly cradled the head of
the "enemy" in her arms. She asked that a priest be summoned, and
presently the young man died in her embrace.

From June 15 through 18, she and her company took back the
towns of Meung, Beaugency and Patay. But these exploits were not
quite as uncomplicated as at Jargeau: the English had received reinforcements, and their army now numbered about five thousand men,
twice as many soldiers as the French. Alençon asked Joan's advice on

how to proceed; practical as always, she replied—perhaps with a smile—"You'll need your spurs." When they approached Beaugency, the English barricaded themselves in the castle. Just then a platoon of soldiers arrived with Arthur de Richemont, the French constable who had fallen out of favor with Charles and his court. They rejected his offer of help, but Joan asked Richemont to swear an oath to the dauphin, and he was allowed to fight once again for France. Soon after, the English surrendered the castle of Beaugency.

This was a terrible personal setback for the Duke of Bedford, brother of the late Henry V, commander of the English forces in France and regent for the boy-king Henry VI. According to Monstrelet, "The English captains in Beaugency saw that this Maiden's fame ... caused them to lose several towns and fortresses, some by attack and conquest, others by [surrender]. Moreover, their men were mostly in a sorry state of fear and seemed to have lost their usual prudence in action." This was at least partly responsible for the overwhelming success of an army of fifteen hundred French assembled at Patay, the next town to be retaken. Almost three thousand English died or were taken prisoner; almost incredibly, the French lost only three men.

With the victory at Patay, the only English field army remaining in France was at last vanquished; the enemy's morale was now low and their tactics disorganized. Still, the war was far from over. Serious challenges lay ahead, and the French cause would experience major setbacks before the English were entirely routed. From this time the Duke of Bedford, a man accustomed to victories on the field and in royal negotiating rooms, cultivated a growing hatred for Joan of Arc that can only be called obsessive.

French confidence had vastly improved and, with it, the will to prevail. Alençon, who had no reason to diminish his own influence and achievements in order to praise Joan, was forthright about her courage and prudence: "It had seemed premature to me to begin the assault [on Jargeau], but Joan said, 'Don't hesitate! This is the hour God has planned for us—

so let us do our task, and God will work on our behalf! . . . Are you afraid?
Don't be—don't you remember that I promised your wife I would bring
you home safe and sound?'"* As for Joan's fears, "She said she was afraid
of nothing except betrayal," a friend recalled.

However we assess the relief of the siege of Orléans and the subsequent successes in the Loire Valley, the military proficiency of the
French shocked the English to the point that French victory now
seemed almost inevitable. If the English had learned that the French
had new *matériel* or a brilliant new commander, they might have been
able to devise counter procedures. But they had underestimated everything, from the loyalty evoked by Joan's leadership at Orléans to the
fresh resolve of the men who knew her. In a way she also stood for
something like a principle of minimal violence, for although she was
always exposed to injury and indeed sustained serious wounds, she
never personally harmed an enemy soldier. The events of the late
spring and early summer of 1429 engendered a new collective spirit
among the French.

With his army now numbered at about twelve thousand, the dauphin at last agreed to go to Reims, where he would be officially anointed and crowned as Charles VII, King of France. This journey was no
simple matter, for the route would take them through territory hostile
to him; nevertheless, the royal caravan set out from Gien on June 29
led by Joan, Alençon, Dunois, her retinue, many captains and commanders, and thousands of knights and men-at-arms. The ardor of the
company may be gauged by the fact that all the men agreed to proceed
as volunteers: the royal treasury did not have a single coin to offer.

Four days before she departed, Joan dictated a letter to the people of
Tournai—still officially a Burgundian stronghold but populated by

---

* Joan and Alençon were already friends, and now his evident trepidation further
evoked her affection; furthermore, the minimal difference in their ages encouraged her
to address him in the familiar *tu* instead of the formal *vous*, which was customary in
addressing a man of his rank.

many loyalists. Obviously she felt that both a warning and an invitation were in order:

> *The Maid sends you the news that in eight days she has chased the English out of every place they held on the river Loire. Many of them are dead or taken prisoners, and they are weary of battle. The Earl of Suffolk, the Lord Talbot, the lord of Scales, and Lord John Fastolf and many knights and captains have been taken, and Suffolk's brother and Glasdale are dead. Hold yourselves fast, loyal Frenchmen, I pray you. And I pray and demand that you be ready to come to the anointing of the gracious King Charles at Reims, where we shall soon be. I commend you to God; may He keep watch over you and give you grace to be able to sustain the cause of the kingdom of France.*

Three days of negotiations in Auxerre brought that town at last within the Valois fold and without open conflict; further along, Troyes, Chalons and Reims pledged their obedience too—although not without some initial resistance from Troyes. Fifteen miles from the city, Joan sent an offer of amnesty and an invitation, dated July 4:

> *Very good and dear friends—lords, townsmen, and residents of the city of Troyes—Joan the Maid commands and informs you on behalf of the King of Heaven our rightful and sovereign Lord, in whose royal service she serves daily, that you should truly obey and recognize the gracious king of France, who will soon be at the city of Reims and at Paris, come what may against him. And with the aid of King Jesus, he will be in all the good cities of this holy kingdom. Loyal Frenchmen, come before King Charles. Do not fail to do so, and have no hesitation about your lives and property. I commend you to God, may God protect you. Reply soon.*

But on July 5, by way of reply, the people of Troyes sent out to Joan an unstable and volatile friar named Richard, who firmly believed that for some reason the world would end the next year. He had been preaching about Joan, telling people that she knew the secrets of God and that she could magically penetrate any city walls. His inference was clear: she might be a witch. "When he came toward me," Joan recalled, "he made the sign of the cross and tossed holy water all around. I said, 'Be brave and approach—I won't fly away!'" Nothing more is known of their meeting, but soon Friar Richard was forbidden to teach and preach.

Troyes decided not to welcome the royal caravan, and the citizens renewed their support for the Anglo-Burgundian cause. Charles called a council, and Joan proposed an immediate attack. When the assault moved forward the next morning, the citizens at once called for negotiations.

As part of her desire to see all Frenchmen unite in support of the new king, Joan sent an invitation to Philip, Duke of Burgundy, who was called "the Good" on account of his vow to go on Crusade against the Turks—a commitment he never honored. Nor did he attend the coronation.

On Saturday, July 16, the people of Reims overwhelmingly abandoned their Anglo-Burgundian loyalty, pledged obedience to Charles, and threw open the gates of the city. At the same time, some lay and clerical English collaborators left Reims. Among them was one of the bishops who had negotiated the infamous Treaty of Troyes, which had denied Charles's legitimacy and promoted England's heirs to the throne of France. The man's name was Pierre Cauchon, and he had been bishop of Beauvais until that city declared its loyalty to Charles. That July he took refuge in Rouen, headquarters of the English presence in France. Cauchon was fiercely Burgundian in his political sympathies. Brilliant and unscrupulous, he was also the former rector of the University of Paris, of whose privileges he was the custodian. Alas, Cauchon eventually masterminded the death of Joan of Arc.

· · ·

THE ROYAL JOURNEY to Reims had been without battle or blood-shed, which seemed another sign of divine favor. In the eyes of the French and even of some Anglo-Burgundians, the presence of Charles and the Maid announced an era of peace. Because Sunday was the tradi-tional day for sacred events, the coronation was held in the cathedral in great haste on Sunday, July 17. The ceremony, which began at nine in the morning and concluded at about two in the afternoon, was a tri-umph of liturgical splendor.

Moments before it began, the Duke of Alençon ritually touched the dauphin's shoulder with a sword and uttered the formula of knight-hood: he was twenty-six years old, but the king-to-be was still not a knight. At the same time, Georges de la Trémoïlle, grand chamberlain of the royal household, assisted Charles as he put on the shoes decorated with fleur-de-lis; onto these Alençon buckled the golden spurs. De la Trémoïlle was also Charles's lieutenant general for Burgundy, an ambi-tious self-promoter and a zealous enemy of Joan and her influence with the king.

The major ceremony began as four lords were chosen to bring from the abbey of Saint-Rémy the sacred oil used for the anointing of Frank-ish kings since the fourth century. According to ancient custom, the four escorts—Gilles de Rais, Jean de Brosse, Jean de Graville, and Louis de Culant—met the humbly barefoot abbot of Saint-Rémy at the door of his abbey. They formed a silent cordon round him and then slowly made their way to the cathedral; at the edge of the sanctuary the abbot handed over the oil to Regnault de Chartres, archbishop of Reims.

Next came the entourage of the royal sword, brought from the abbey of Saint-Denis, near Paris—but secretly because the region was still controlled by Anglo-Burgundian captains. The blade was engraved with fleur-de-lis from hilt to point, and the sword was held aloft in pro-cession to the altar by the favorite nephew of Georges de la Trémoïlle.

Following that was the procession of six peers who (imitating the rit-ual of Clovis) were to hold the crown above Charles's head before the actual coronation. The men for the task that day were Alençon; the counts of Clermont, Vendôme and Laval; Raoul de Gaucourt (captain of Orléans); and Georges de la Trémoïlle. This procession also included six bishops, but three had to be replaced because they were fiercely anti-Valois and hence were absent. One of those three was Pierre Cauchon.

In the tradition of the anointing of the ancient kings of Israel (especially David), Charles was anointed on his chest, shoulders, elbows, and wrists by the archbishop of Reims, his body thus consecrated to the service of God and the people. The king was the lieutenant of God in matters temporal; more than anyone, he was the servant and leader of the French people, as much chosen by God as Israel of old had been. Charles swore to honor "justice and the law" and to defend Church and people, especially the poor and disenfranchised, from all enemies.

The archbishop then escorted Charles to the main altar, where his head was anointed and a ring was slipped onto his right index finger, symbol of the union between the king and his people. To the accompaniment of the blast of trumpets and the cheers of everyone in the cathedral, the crown was then lowered onto Charles's head. At last he was no longer the dauphin but Charles VII, the consecrated, true, and legitimate king of France.

Wearing armor and bearing her banner, Joan stood nearby throughout the ceremony. Why did she bring her personal standard? "It had endured very much," she said later, "and it was only fair that it should share in the honor."* Her presence must have impressed everyone in the cathedral, for the coronation vindicated a woman, who would normally have been held suspect in the male world of court, army and clergy. Perhaps most among the worshippers, the honor was shared by five people who stood near Joan and whose pride we may only imagine—her parents, who had come from Domrémy; her brothers Jean

---

* The absence of Charles's wife, Marie of Anjou, is easily explained: the route to Reims was dangerous, and the army feared for her safety. In addition, the coronation of the French queen consort had far less significance than in earlier times.

and Pierre; and Durand Laxart, her first advocate and helper. The financial records of Reims testify to their attendance, adding that the city
paid for their lodging at an inn across the cathedral square.

Her family's presence may well have inspired Joan when the king
asked if she wished a favor on this great occasion. She begged nothing
for herself, she replied, but she requested that the people of Domrémy
and of neighboring Greux might henceforth have the privilege of tax-
free status. This the king gladly bestowed two weeks later, as a surviving document reveals. Beside the royal decree, written in Charles's own
hand, is a simple explanation of the exemption: "*Rien—la Pucelle:*
Nothing [in taxes], [it was for] the Maid."

ON CORONATION DAY Joan dictated a letter to Philip the Good,
Duke of Burgundy, still an enemy of the king:

> *Most high and noble prince, the Maid summons you—by my sover-
> eign Lord the King of Heaven—to make a lasting peace with the king of
> France. Each of you must pardon the other fully and sincerely, as loyal
> Christians should. If it pleases you to make war, go and do so against the
> Saracens.* Prince of Burgundy, I beg you: make no more war on France.
> Withdraw at once your men who do so. As for my gentle king of France,
> he is ready to make peace with you.... You will win no more battles
> against loyal Frenchmen, and all who do so are warring against King
> Jesus, King of Heaven and earth. I pray you, with my hands joined, not
> to seek battle or war.... I wrote to you, inviting you to the coronation—
> but I have had no reply, nor have I heard any news of the herald whom I
> sent to you with that message. I commend you to God ... and I pray God
> that He will establish a good peace.*

---

* There is a touch of sarcasm here: for years Philip had repeated his unfulfilled vow to
join a Crusade. If he truly wanted to make war, Joan advised him to do it as promised—against infidels, not the French.

The letter, as one historian has written, "evokes the grandeur of Joan's Christian, martial, and chivalric mentality at the same time that it [indicates] the increasing irrelevance of these qualities to her world and moment." The letter also reveals Joan's poignant unawareness of the political machinations then driving powerful men among the English, their Burgundian allies, and the French. Not long after, a two-week truce was declared between the king and the duke. Philip said he would turn Paris over to the king after that period, but of course he intended no such thing; instead, he used the time to shore up his defense of the capital.

As these intrigues were taking shape, Joan was being celebrated in a long poem by Christine de Pisan, a prolific author who wrote courtly love poems, a life of Charles V and books about heroic women. Her last work, almost certainly written during the week of July 23–31, was "Le Ditié de Jehanne d'Arc" (The Story of Joan of Arc), an extended lyric in praise of the Maid's achievements.

It is a fact well worth remembering that God has wished to bestow such great blessings on France through a young virgin.... And you, Charles, King of France, see your honor exalted by the Maid who has laid low your enemies.... And all this has been brought about by the intelligence of the Maid who, God be thanked, has played her part in this matter.... And you, blessed Maid, you untied the rope which held France so tightly bound....

Blessed be He who created you, Joan, Maiden sent from God.... Moses miraculously and indefatigably led God's people out of Egypt. In the same way, blessed Maid, you have led us out of evil.... And the prowess of all the great men of the past cannot be compared to this woman's, whose concern it is to cast out our enemies. This is God's doing: it is He who guides her and who has given her a heart greater than that of any man....

I have heard of Esther, Judith, and Deborah, women of great worth, through whom God delivered His people from oppression,

and I have heard of many other women as well, champions every one
of them, through whom He performed many miracles—but He has
accomplished more through this Maid. Her achievement is no illusion, for she was carefully put to the test in council and well examined. But she was destined to accomplish her mission. Whatever
she does, she always has her eyes fixed on God; nowhere does her
devotion ever falter. What honor for the female sex, that the kingdom is now recovered and made safe by a woman—something that
five thousand men could not have done.... This is God's doing: it is
He who leads her. Before all the brave men of the past, this woman
must wear the crown—and she has not yet accomplished her whole
mission! But destroying the English race is not her main concern—
it is rather to ensure the survival of the faith....

"Her main concern is to ensure the survival of the faith." This was
not merely the poetic hyperbole of Christine de Pisan; it was implicit in
everything Joan of Arc did. To modern ears that might seem quite a
leap: how can the expulsion of the English and the survival of France be
identified with preserving faith?

At this point it is crucial to keep in mind that Joan's goal of saving
France was, she claimed, God's own will. Referring constantly to divine
guidance, she insisted that she did nothing but what was directed. If
her spiritual experience may be trusted as valid, then she was right in
her assertion that France was a sacred nation that had to be saved.

As Siobhan Nash-Marshall has suggested in an important scholarly article, more than physical or psychological causes must be found
if one is to challenge her claim and explore the notion of sacred
nations. Some critics have insisted that Ménière's disease (a condition
affecting the ear or ears) or a neoplasm of the brain or frank psycho-
sis was the cause of her voices and visions. But people with Ménière's
disease, with its attendant vertigo, impaired hearing and imbalance,

cannot ride horses for days, nor can they leap into battle, climb ladders, and otherwise lead extremely active lives without interruption.

As for a benign or malignant brain tumor, such a condition becomes progressively worse and brings with it alarming and debilitating symptoms, such as violent vomiting, loss of sight, irrational behavior, blindness, incapacitating headaches, and partial paralysis. Joan experienced none of these frightful signs, and her physical activity was interrupted only briefly by war wounds, not by any organic illness.

Similarly, schizophrenia or other forms of grave mental illness simply do not appear in the life of this unlettered girl whose manner, convictions and logic were enough to convince a king to assign her to a critical job with soldiers. Had she seemed unbalanced, no responsible royal or noble would have allowed her to advise and to lead the very fighters, mercenaries and volunteers on whom they depended for their kingdom; nor would worldly men like Metz, Poulengy, Alençon, Dunois, La Hire and the rest have so readily trusted and attached themselves to her. Men liked and admired her; they did not hold her in suspicion.

Nor did Joan give any indications of being a disturbed girl: she spoke calmly, with logic and unshakable faith. She argued with educated councilors and learned churchmen, and her responses showed only a natural cleverness, a quick and rational mind, a healthy self-confidence, a keen sense of humor and a strong sense of the realities of what had happened, was happening and might happen. Her actions with others, in other words, reveal a young woman who did not live in a world of fantasy or illusion.

Perhaps most important, we must keep in mind that Joan had no training in such things as court procedures, military maneuvers, battle horsemanship, weaponry or the fine points of theological or legal disputes. That she acquitted herself so brilliantly in these areas may not be credited to Ménière's disease, a brain tumor or an unbalanced mind.

Among the hundreds of witnesses to her achievements and the hundreds more who knew her during her lifetime, not a single person alluded to anything like physical, emotional or mental illness. The unanimous sense of those present was that she was a remarkably normal young woman who was able to achieve remarkably memorable deeds at the age of seventeen.

Joan's claim that God had France in His care because France was sacred to Him may not be merely a medieval trope, embarrassingly old-fashioned language that today we must expunge from our vocabularies. To claim that France is sacred does not imply that *only* France is sacred. Throughout history, men and women have arisen everywhere who testify to the sacredness of nations. Perhaps today more than ever, we are aware that the identity and integrity of nations are supremely significant for the human race—that the facile invasion of a sovereign state and genocide are abhorrent.

In this regard, the entire Jewish-Christian faith tradition is based on the belief that God once summoned ordinary people and *through them* worked extraordinary deeds for His own purpose, which is to bring all peoples to Himself. Abraham, Isaac, Jacob, Moses and the prophets were but a few of those called to establish and save the nation of Israel. But Israel was brought into existence and later triumphed over its enemies not only for its own sake. This is made clear throughout the Hebrew Scriptures: God saved that nation so that *all* nations might be embraced. Israel was to be "a light to the gentiles," as both Old and New Testaments reiterate. God chose the Israelites not to dominate or control but rather to serve others. The Christian Scriptures make the point more specific: the gentiles are not excluded from God's embrace, for the light of Israel shines on the gentiles and shows the way into that embrace. All the peoples of the world are to be brought into the capacious light of the knowledge of God's friendship. Nowhere is it implied that the nation of Israel, or any other nation, should cease to exist.

Because no single person or group represents everything it means to be human, it is the variety of people within a nation that gives it an irreplaceable, unique character—its "national personality." As with individuals, so with nations: it is the diversity of peoples that furthers the process of the world. Although many nations have tried, none may set itself up as the only or the predominant nation, forcing its culture, ideology, religion or political agenda on any other nation. For Joan of Arc, this was precisely what England was trying to do through its nobles, armies and war machinery. France deserved its identity and, as a symbol of its people, the king.

FOUR DAYS AFTER the coronation, Charles embarked on a royal tour, presenting himself to his people and receiving their formal acts of loyalty and submission. Never a decisive man in military matters, he temporized by listening to men who disliked Joan, while she and Alençon urged him to capitalize on the recent victories as well as the prestige afforded by coronation. The English had lost both numbers and morale, and Joan and her partners insisted that now was the time to recapture Paris and reunite the French people; otherwise recent triumphs could be reduced to insignificance.

But Charles preferred to bide his time, waiting for Philip of Burgundy to turn over Paris peacefully. The coronation had no transforming effect on the king's self-awareness, for although Paris was now his city, he was hesitant to take it. Instead of advancing on Paris, the royal entourage headed northwest to Corbeny, then south to Soissons, Château-Thierry, Monmirail and Provins.

Charles's optimism was in vain. The truce Philip proposed was merely a pretext to seal off as much of Paris as possible so that it would not fall to the king. This Joan suspected, as she wrote in a letter dictated from Provins to the people of Reims on August 5:

My dear friends in Reims, Joan the Maid greets you and asks that you have no concerns about the good cause she pursued on behalf of the royal house. I promise that I will never abandon you as long as I live. It's true that the king has made a fifteen-day truce with the Duke of Burgundy, who is then supposed to turn over Paris peacefully. But don't be surprised if I don't enter Paris so quickly. I really don't like truces made like this, and I don't know if I can support them—but if I do so, it will only be to protect the king's honor. I shall maintain the king's army so as to be ready if the Burgundians aren't true to their word. So my dear friends, do not worry so long as I live, but keep good watch and defend [Reims], and let me know if any traitors seek to harm you. Let me have some news of you. I commend you to God—may He protect you.

Joan was unaware that the Duke of Bedford, in particular, was moving to support Philip's betrayal of the truce because he sought an end to the meddlesome Maid who had sabotaged English supremacy. Bedford and Philip, often hostile to each other, were united on the matter of Joan. Their diplomatic entente was helped by the fact that Bedford had married Philip's sister.

Bedford maneuvered quickly: he summoned to his side a number of soldiers who had been sent to fight heretics in Bohemia, thus in effect turning his campaign into a crusade, a sacred venture against heretics. Their target, Bedford wrote to the king of France in a tone astonishingly disrespectful, was Joan herself—a heretic and, because she beguiled and corrupted the goals of good Christian men, a witch. "You seduce and abuse the ignorant and rely on the assistance of the superstitious and reprobate, and even of that deranged and infamous woman who goes about in men's clothes and is of dissolute conduct."

There was no evidence for heresy, but Bedford was certain that he and his Burgundian bishops could contrive a rationale for condemning her if she could be captured and put on trial. Those goals seemed achievable, and then it would be a short route to her execution, the complete demolition of French morale, the defeat of Charles VII, and—voilà!—the eight-year-old Henry VI of England would also become king of France.

At the same time, Georges de la Trémoïlle was making every effort to poison Charles against Joan, and in his perfidy he exploited Charles's wife and mother-in-law. Of Joan, la Trémoïlle wrote to them, "She leaves no doubt that she will bring Paris under her control"—not the control of France, not that of the king, but *her* control.

As she had said, Joan feared only treason, and now she sensed the proximate reality of it. Most poignant of all, her voices seemed no longer to provide clear direction as to her future activities with the king, and this she took to mean that her military career was drawing to a close.

SEVEN

A Leap of Faith

(August 1429–December 1430)

By the time the royal expedition arrived at Crépy-en-Valois on Thursday, August 11, Joan sensed that forces both English and French were seeking her disgrace and demise. She had won the king's approval; she had earned the loyalty and respect of noblemen and battle leaders; and she had won the admiration and affection of soldiers and ordinary citizens. How could such enmity on the part of a few so suddenly become so potent?

The French too had their cunning and formidable men, such as la Trémoïlle, the king's chamberlain and his chief negotiator with Burgundy, to whom Charles owed vast sums of money and whose counsel, therefore, he could not reject outright. La Trémoïlle's scheme, which he recommended daily to the king, was to maintain a truce between French and Burgundian troops and then hire foreign soldiers to battle the English. There was no place in la Trémoïlle's plan for the likes of Joan, who rightly distrusted the idea of a truce and recommended acting at once to retake Paris for the anointed king. The chamberlain wanted her dismissed and sent home, but the king was not ready to do so; she was an asset, at least in what passed for his public relations, and he wanted to keep her a while longer. It is unclear whether

Charles knew that la Trémoïlle was sowing the seeds of suspicion about Joan among those at court as well as with the queen and her mother.

In addition, those who proclaimed themselves friends of the king were furtively making deals with both the Burgundians and the English, for they realized that alliance with England, even now, would offer them large financial advantages. The coffers of Charles VII were virtually empty, but the situation across the channel was quite different. These conspirators also felt that England would eventually prevail, and they wanted to be on the winning side. Their traitorous collaboration represented the most perfidious era in French history until the Nazi occupation and the Vichy government, to which this period bears several unfortunate similarities.

Joan was rigorously unique—not a queen, a mother, an aristocrat, a nun, or an intellectual but a woman of action and profound religious faith, convinced that God willed the integrity of her country. In other words, her clarity and simplicity put to shame all the wily, selfish politicians and conniving churchmen doing business with them, who finally decided that she had outlived her usefulness and had to go.

The faculty of the University of Paris was also involved. Theologians, philosophers, and clergy in the capital were impatient to eradicate Joan's influence and to have her silenced. A number of professors signed a letter to none other than the pope, in which they charged Joan with rank heresy; their primary accusation was that she claimed to know the future. Such academic involvement was not as surprising as it may seem today, for the University of Paris presented itself to the world as the intellectual guardian of orthodoxy, standing ready to condemn anyone who spoke or acted in God's name without seeking its approval. In addition, the university faculty championed the Treaty of Troyes and endorsed an English king on the throne of France as the shortest route to peace. Their position was virtually a legal judgment, and it carried great weight all over France: according to these august men, Joan of Arc was a dangerous charlatan.

• • •

BEFORE THE SUMMER of 1429 was over, the representatives of Philip of Burgundy were quietly negotiating with the Duke of Bedford about a hypothetical price to be paid for handing over Joan of Arc if she could be captured. There was something almost fateful about her, the English decided, something that seemed to be the devil's own work. She must be a witch to have accomplished so much, to have secured such loyalty from troops—and witches must be eliminated from the world. Precisely at this point in the fifteenth century, belief in witchcraft reached a pitch of frenzy hitherto unknown: religious folk were terrified of those considered witches, and clergymen were hunting down countless innocent women in the belief that they consorted with or were tools of demonic powers.

A great deal had to be demonstrated, however. And Joan could not be put on trial and executed by an English court merely for succeeding in battle and routing English plans. She would have to be condemned by an ecclesiastical court for reasons of witchcraft and heresy; alas, an ecclesiastical court favorable to England and ready to accept cash and favors for the deed would be readily available.

Joan read the prevailing winds, believed that her task for France was complete, and wanted to go home. "I wish it were God's will for me to go away now," she said to Dunois in August, "and to lay down my armor and return to serving my parents by looking after the flocks with my sister and brothers, who would be so happy to have me at home." Poignantly, Joan spoke of her "sister and brothers" and life at home as it had been before her brothers joined her in battle and her sister died.

Although she had spent only five months in royal circles and two months in the thick of warfare, she understood that now her real troubles would begin, and she longed to avoid them. In Reims, her farewell to her family as they returned to Domrémy must have been difficult for them all; now more than ever, she missed life at home. Disillusionment followed disappointment from the summer of 1429 to the spring of 1430, for Joan had made it possible for Charles to be anointed king, and now he was the most acute source of her regret. Not that she would have reversed the coronation, and not that she lamented any moment of battle, but Charles preferred not to face the unpleasant realities at hand, and Joan preferred to confront them promptly.

Apparently she was of two minds. On the one hand, she became ever more anguished and depressed over the apathy of the king and the foolish and often treacherous counsel he heeded—hence her wish to return to Domrémy. But on the other hand, she saw how much might be done, with proper troops, to effect a rapid departure of the English from French soil. Most of all, she grew angry and impatient at the king's inclination to grasp at every diplomatic straw thrown at him by the wily Philip of Burgundy.

Charles still hoped that Philip would simply surrender Paris to him. Reluctantly, however, he provided some troops to attend Joan and Alençon in an attempt to recapture the city on September 8. "The Maid took her standard in hand," according to Perceval de Cagny, the duke's squire and chronicler,

and the assault was hard and long, lasting from about two in the afternoon until nightfall. After the sun had set, the Maid was hit by a crossbow bolt in her thigh. After she had been hit, she insisted even more strenuously that everyone should approach the walls so that the place would be taken. But because it was night and she was wounded and the men-at-arms were weary from the day-long assault, Gaucourt and others came to the Maid and, against her will, carried her away. And so the assault ended.

Joan agreed to take but one night's rest, and then she told the astonished Alençon that she was ready to resume with another plan of attack the following day. The troops rallied, but then messengers from the king arrived, ordering Joan and the duke to meet him at Saint-Denis. The king ordered the army to abandon the attack on Paris, and he went back to Gien, in the Loire Valley; there he formally disbanded his troops and announced that henceforth he would pursue only a reconciliation with Philip—an expectation that everyone but the king knew was both futile and dangerous.

After her meeting with the king at Saint-Denis, Joan went to the chapel royal, where she left her armor and sword—the traditional gesture of thanksgiving for surviving a recent war wound. But it is also the sign by which a soldier acknowledges that the battles are over, the race run. Joan had effected Charles's coronation, and now he was her king; she may well have thought that with the formal disbanding of the royal army she would henceforth be without purpose to the man she had brought to the throne, and therefore to the country.

Because he was a nobleman, Jean d'Alençon did not require the king's permission to raise troops and go to battle—which is just what he proposed that autumn when he invited Joan to accompany him on a campaign to Normandy, which was Burgundian territory. But Charles was persuaded by la Trémoïlle not to permit this, in order to avoid provoking the Burgundians while negotiations continued on yet another truce with Philip (despite the fact that he had failed to yield Paris after the first truce). "The Maid remained much annoyed at the king," wrote Alençon's chronicler.

That situation was aggravated by Charles's decision to prevent any further possible undertakings between the Maid and the duke; this he accomplished by a formal instruction that Joan and Alençon were never to meet again. No doubt he envied their accomplishments, which highlighted his own inefficiency and weakness. By severing this friendship, the king also ensured that any troops under their separate commands would be weakened. This, of course, was exactly what men like la Trémoïlle wanted, for Charles had neither the inclination nor the talent for military strategy. And so the Maid and her "fair duke," good friends and comrades-in-arms, were never reunited.

BY THE AUTUMN of 1429 Joan felt utterly useless. Charles commanded her presence at court, in Gien and elsewhere, and there she resided in comfortable indolence—not without complaining of her inactivity—in quarters provided for herself, her staff and her two brothers. At the home of the king's finance minister (where she was treated for her leg injury), Joan was often besieged by people who wanted her to bless rosary beads and other pious objects by touching them. "Touch them yourselves," she said with a laugh. "Your touch will do as much good as mine!" She had no desire to be considered an object of veneration.

In November, probably at la Trémoïlle's instigation, the king decided to send Joan to battle in order to avoid her interference in the ongoing but futile negotiations with Burgundy. She was given troops for an assault on Saint-Pierre-le-Moûtier, southeast of Bourges, where the English swiftly capitulated.

But at the next offensive, La Charité, a Burgundian town crucial to the king's protection, Joan's forces were few. Like all leaders of battle during the Hundred Years' War, she had to beg for help from neighboring towns and aristocrats. "To my dear and good friends at Riom," she dictated in a letter,

> You well know how the town of Saint-Pierre-le-Moûtier was taken by assault, and with God's help I intend to clear out the other places which are against the king. But because so much gunpowder, projectiles and other war materials had been expended before this town, and because I and the lords who are here are so poorly supplied for laying siege to La Charité, where we will be going shortly, I pray you, upon whatever love you have for the well-being and honor for the king and also all the others

here, that you will immediately send and donate for the siege gunpowder, saltpeter, sulfur, projectiles, arbalests [crossbow catapults] and other materials of war.

Joan's signature was obviously her own, for it came from one who was just learning to write: the letters are wobbly, and the initial *J* of her name resembles the number seven.

Contributions and reinforcements from Riom never arrived, and Joan had to beg Charles for help. Finally she abandoned the attack "because the king did not raise funds to send her either supplies or money to maintain her company," wrote one witness. "She had to raise the siege and withdraw in great displeasure."

At Christmas the king announced the ennoblement of Joan, her family and their descendants. "We desire to offer thanks," the decree stated, "for the many remarkable benefits of divine largesse that have been accorded us through the agency of the Maid, Jeanne d'Ay [sic] de Domrémy ... [and] we consider also the laudable, graceful, and effective services already rendered by the aforesaid Jeanne in every way, to us and to our kingdom...." On the coat of arms were two gold lilies and between them a sword supporting a crown, the symbolic rendering of what Joan had done for France. It was very much a farewell gesture to a woman, like a gift to a retiring employee. Joan's rank, of which she never spoke, was essentially that of a *comtesse*, similar to an English marchioness or countess. Her family received the surname du Lys, from the lilies on their emblem.

This was a crafty deed. By any measure, the king could not be faulted for a lack of gratitude to one so widely admired. But at the same time, ennoblement had an important effect on Joan. Like Alençon and others, she no longer required the king's permission to raise troops and wage war, for nobles could do this entirely on their own. But if she did in fact go to battle, she would be completely responsible for its consequences; in effect, Charles was separating himself from her. He did not want her to act or lead in his name or beneath his banner. She had saved Orléans and the monarchy, and now she had the eminence of a noblewoman. Thank you, Joan, and good-bye: that was essentially the king's mind.

Thus began a cold and lonely winter, which Joan spent mostly at Sully-sur-Loire, in a castle belonging to la Trémoïlle's family, who were not warm hosts. In addition to her somber inactivity and her separation from those she loved and trusted in and out of the army, she was also denied the consolation of her voices, which now seemed to fall silent. She prayed and maintained a composed stillness as much as possible, but there was no clear indication of her future. For perhaps the first time, Joan of Arc knew the kind of spiritual darkness that is part of the experience of everyone who seeks God.

IN THE SPRING of 1430, with the king's tacit approval, she proceeded north with a company of about three hundred fifty mercenary men-at-arms, prepared to defeat an enemy offensive against the town of Compiègne, fifty miles north of Paris. There resistance to the occupation and loyalty to Charles were strongly entrenched, and so a turning back of the Anglo-Burgundians would provide another opportunity to move forward and seize the capital, thus repeating the success of Orléans.

On the way she tried to take a Burgundian post at Margny. As so often, Joan outfitted herself colorfully, the better to be seen by her soldiers. "She mounted her horse armed as would a man," recalled none other than the Burgundian chronicler Chastellain,

> adorned with a doublet of rich cloth-of-gold over her breastplate. She rode a very handsome, proud gray courser and displayed herself in her armor and her bearing as a captain would have done ... and in that array, with her standard raised high and fluttering in

the wind, and well accompanied by many noble men, she sallied forth from the city, about four hours past midday.

Her effort failed, for the enemy's forces comprised about six thousand men.

On May 14 Joan tried to isolate Philip's advance to Compiègne by taking a bridge to the town. At first it seemed as if she would succeed, but fresh reinforcements arrived for the Burgundians. Proceeding by another route, Joan led her troops into Compiègne on the morning of May 23. Next day, she and the men successfully took the camp at Margny.

Enemy soldiers, meanwhile, had virtually surrounded the town—a force quickly augmented by the troops of Jean de Luxembourg, a Burgundian ambassador who was captain of a company and ferociously devoted to Philip of Burgundy. When the French soldiers saw that they were now perilously outnumbered, they retreated to Compiègne—courageously covered at the end of their line by Joan, who always placed herself in the most dangerous positions, at the head of an entry into battle or at the rear guard covering a retreat. Most of her troops entered swiftly and safely into the town precincts.

Then things happened quickly, as the hunter and the hunted finally met at the foot of the bridge into Compiègne. "During that time," as a witness recalled, "the captain of [the town], seeing the great multitude of Burgundians and Englishmen ready to get on the bridge ... raised the drawbridge of the city and closed the gate. So the Maid was shut outside, and only a few of her men were with her." Those few included her faithful squire Jean d'Aulon, her brother Pierre, the faithful Louis de Coutes and several others who had been with her since Orléans and whose names are lost to us.

Even the Burgundian Chastellain admired Joan and seemed to take pity on her predicament: "The Maid performed a great feat and took much pain to save her company from loss, staying behind like a chief and like the most valiant member of the flock." But an enemy archer named Lyonnel caught up with her, "laid hold of her from the side by her cloth-of-gold doublet, and pulled her from her horse to the ground." He then handed her over to one of Jean de Luxembourg's lieutenants, who had hastened to the spot for the ritual of surrender, demanding Joan's capitulation and her oath of loyalty. She protested loudly that she had sworn her faith to another. From that moment, late in the afternoon of Tuesday, May 23, 1430, Joan was a prisoner, and so she remained for the rest of her life.

AT FIRST SHE was a war hostage, in captivity to Jean de Luxembourg, an Anglo-Burgundian loyal to his overlord Philip the Good and a counselor to the king of England, whose treasury paid him a monthly stipend. "By the pleasure of our blessed Creator," wrote Philip triumphantly to the duke of Savoy, "the woman called the Maid has been taken, and from her capture will be recognized the error and mad belief of all those who become sympathetic and favorable to the deeds of this woman."

The lawyers and doctors at the University of Paris chimed in too—with a letter to Philip:

> Since all loyal Christian princes and all other true Catholics are held to the duty of extirpating all errors against the faith and the scandal that follows such errors among simple Christian folk, and since it is a matter of common knowledge that diverse errors have been sown and published in many cities, towns and other places by a certain woman named Joan, whom the adversaries of this kingdom call the Maid ... we beseech you ... that as soon as it can be done safely and conveniently, the aforesaid Joan be brought under our jurisdiction as a prisoner, since she is strongly suspected of various crimes smacking of heresy, so as to appear before us and a procurator of the Holy Inquisition.

On Wednesday, May 24, the morning after her capture, Joan, along with Jean d'Aulon and her brother, Pierre, were dispatched to a fortress just northeast of Compiègne, at Clairoix. Three days later Jean de Luxembourg decided to secure the prisoners in his own castle at Beaulieu-lès-Fontaines, where he expected to receive immediate offers of a very high ransom.

Captivity was unpleasant, but the humane customs regarding war prisoners were observed. No one in the group was subjected to harsh treatment, and no immediate threats were made to their lives. In addition, they had every reason to expect imminent freedom: the standard procedure in such cases was to demand from a prestigious captive's allies a ransom, which, once paid, secured release. For Joan the only potential hazard at Beaulieu was the presence of a small platoon of rough Burgundian mercenaries, who came and went, breathing threats and brandishing weapons.

On June 6 she was transported for a day to the bishop's palace at near-by Noyon, where she was presented to two visitors—Philip of Burgundy and his wife, Isabelle. There is no record of the exchange between the duke and the Maid, but it was most likely not an interrogation but merely a chance for Philip to satisfy his curiosity with a glimpse and a brief conversation. His wife liked, admired and sympathized with Joan, and she tried to persuade her husband not to sell her to the English, or at least to guarantee the safety of her captivity by having her moved to their castle at Beaurevoir, a more hospitable place (at least for a captive). During the following weeks the matter was discussed with Jean de Luxembourg, and the transfer was eventually effected.

However, before that move, drama ensued. Joan's room at Beaulieu lay in the center of the octagonal castle. Jailers were stationed nearby, but Jean d'Aulon was permitted to attend her, and she was not subjected to molestation or harassment. When she learned that her removal to Beaurevoir would mean her separation from d'Aulon and her brother, she hatched an idea. "Help yourself and God will help you" had always been one of her mottoes; in fact, she used those very words in French.

One night in early July she noticed that the wooden planks on her floor had been poorly joined. Working quietly, strengthened by battle, she tore away enough of the wood to lower herself to the room beneath, which was near the main entrance. Adjacent to the massive door was a room for sentries, who were sleeping, with the key to their room hanging on the outside of the door. As she tried to lock in the men before making her escape, guards on night patrol saw her and called out, thus thwarting her getaway. She was then placed in a more secure room.

At the same time, the faculty at the University of Paris repeated its insistence on having Joan within its jurisdiction. The representative of that community was Pierre Cauchon, who regarded Joan as his archenemy for, as bishop of Beauvais, he had been forced into exile when that city proclaimed its loyalty to Charles during the postcoronation tour. Cauchon happened to be in Normandy when Joan was captured, and now he lived in Rouen, England's French headquarters. But he was not bishop of that city; at that time the post was vacant. Always a devious politician with his eye on both royal and financial favors, he at once conferred with Bedford on the most expeditious way of having Joan delivered to them. If he could successfully manage the trial and have her dispatched, he could anticipate many royal rewards—among them the wealthy bishopric of Rouen.

Cauchon was a man to reckon with. Former rector of the University of Paris, he was then about sixty years old and had climbed relentlessly —even ruthlessly—up the ladder of parochial and canonical appointments. He had been canon of Reims, Chartres, Châlons and Beauvais and was close to Pope Martin V, whose election he had supported. Cauchon had served the interests of England since 1420, had helped to draft the language of the Treaty of Troyes against France, and was charged with the matter of Joan of Arc.

An offer was made to Jean de Luxembourg—not for ransom (which would mean her freedom to return to the service of France), but for an outright purchase of the Maid as an object the English desired to possess and would then, of course, have the Church condemn for heresy. There was no such thing as separation of church and state, and anyone could be tried in an Inquisition for a religious crime or public sin and then turned over to the secular arm for execution. In Joan's case the charge of heresy meant that the ecclesiastical court would act under the aegis of the Inquisition, which worked to uphold the articles of faith and punish those who violated them. The more noteworthy the prisoner, the more necessary it was to deal firmly, and as everyone knew even then, Joan would never have been subjected to a trial if she had been on the side of the English. She was, to put it succinctly, a political pawn destined to die on fabricated charges of religious impropriety—a predicament much like that of Jesus Christ.

Most important, if Joan were brought to trial and found guilty of heresy, the coronation of Charles would be entirely discredited and his kingship essentially invalidated. The enemy counted on Charles's vacillation to make this an easy reality.

Furthermore, the doctors of the university and their affiliated clergy would do more than ingratiate themselves with the English by providing an excuse to get rid of Joan: they would, in the bargain, exercise their power over a famous, influential, and much-admired woman. Joan relied on prayer and her experience of God's proximity to determine her choices and her vocation, and such an independent spirit was a source of outrage to cherished institutional prerogatives. In this regard Joan of Arc must be regarded as one who, however indeliberately, battled institutional and clerical domination as much as she fought the occupying armies of England.

The Anglo-Burgundian men believed that Joan had to be permanently excised from the world. To that end, Cauchon bid ten thousand gold *écus*, the maximum paid by a king to buy a prisoner from one of his vassals (in modern terms, about half a million dollars). There was no counteroffer, and thus the long interval between Cauchon's offer in early July and the conclusion of the sale in December may seem hard to understand. But the wives of Burgundy and Luxembourg were gently and firmly pressuring their husbands not to act hastily in the matter of turning Joan over to the English, no matter the money to be realized.

At her trial Joan specifically mentioned Luxembourg's wife as sympathetic during her months at Beaurevoir, where she arrived sometime in late July or early August and where the duke's aunt and stepdaughter were also friendly toward her—all of them Armagnac loyalists (and all named Jeanne). As for the duke himself, it is reasonable to think that he too liked her and came to believe that she was sent by God; if the latter, then he would have been terrified to seek her destruction. Luxembourg made no reply to Cauchon's two offers in May and July; instead he waited in vain for the king himself to ransom the young woman who had made the coronation possible.

But Charles was impervious to the entreaties of those who wished Joan ransomed. Some claimed he had not the money, but that is a specious argument for he could have raised it in a week by letters asking for contributions. More to the point, his troops had captured the Earl of Suffolk, whose freedom could have been exchanged for hers. But the king did nothing.

Joan's family could not afford the huge ransom set for her. The freedom of her few companions and of her brothers was purchased for a nominal fee by their comrades-in-arms; they were not, after all, significant prisoners. That Joan's troops elsewhere did not act similarly on her behalf was due to the fact that her "army," such as it had been, was now widely scattered. The ransom also lay far beyond the abilities of Alençon, Dunois and others, who doubtless presumed the king would act properly and promptly on Joan's behalf. As for the people of

Orléans, they were too poor even to ransom their own duke, who had been imprisoned in England for fifteen years.

The king's failure to act may have been due at least partly to his mercurial attitude toward friends and supporters, whom he often raised high one week and exiled the next. In addition, Joan and her troops had failed in the siege of Paris: was she a false prophet after all, and if not, would she somehow be rescued by God? It is possible also that Charles feared Joan's return, for if she engaged in further successful military exploits and her popularity grew accordingly, he might appear even more impotent, with his temporizing truces and ineffectual negotiations.

The king knew the Maid well enough to know that she did not work for her own glory or advancement, but la Trémoïlle and company did everything they could to poison him against Joan. They knew Charles was careful to cultivate his own eminence; indeed, after the coronation he'd had countless medals struck with his own image and the legend "Charles the Triumphant." The king may not have regretted seeing the last of the young woman to whom he owed so much.

On a deeper level, Charles's inertia on Joan's behalf raises the possibility that he never really believed in the reality of Joan's spiritual claims, much less in God's guidance of her and of France. Had he done so, the king would scarcely have treated her so shabbily. His failure to act for her safety was, in a tragic sense, the logical term of his disinclination to follow her advice about so many campaigns—and indeed his reluctance to say or do anything she recommended. His reasonable hesitation when she first came to him at Chinon seems to have developed into a chronic skepticism, and his ennoblement of her had been a shrewd way of separating himself from her. To put the matter briefly, the dauphin-become-king seems not to have taken Joan of Arc very seriously.

The English and Burgundians, by contrast, assessed Joan far more earnestly, to the point of spending a great deal of money and effort to orchestrate a momentous juridical process to discount her, her claims and thus the king she championed. Bedford and company understood that if Joan had been sent by God, then the English cause in France was doomed and their eternal salvation in terrifying jeopardy. They had to demonstrate that Joan was not God's messenger, that France's security did not matter in the divine economy, and that God wanted England on French soil. That is why the trial had to be an Inquisition. Here lies one of the ironies of Joan of Arc: that her enemies made more of her than did her king.

Cauchon, meantime, was busy negotiating, being handsomely paid for his time and reimbursed for his travel expenses. He signed a document preserved in the British Royal Archives declaring his receipt of monies "for service to the King [of England] in several journeys, going to the Duke of Burgundy or to John of Luxembourg in Flanders, to Compiègne, to Beaurevoir, all in the matter of Joan, called the Maid." On July 14, for example, he visited Jean de Luxembourg with letters of summons from the University of Paris, demanding Joan's release to him: "The woman commonly called Joan the Maid, now prisoner, must be sent to the King [of England] to be delivered over to the Church for trial, because she is suspected of many crimes, sorceries, idolatry, intercourse with demons, and other matters relative to faith and against faith."

By late autumn Charles's silence and the lack of any offer or counteroffer for Joan placed Luxembourg in an impossible position, and he could no longer delay her sale to the English. Philip of Burgundy, his overlord, was awaiting news of Luxembourg's decision, as was Bedford. Personal feeling about Joan or sympathy for her or a sense that his family might be quite right about her—these could no longer allow him to ignore the English offer.

THAT AUTUMN OF 1430, when it became clear that she would indeed be sold to the English, Joan acted desperately. There was a seventy-foot drop from her tower keep to the ground, and she jumped from her cell. "I heard that the good people of Compiègne would be put to fire and sword ... and that was one of the reasons I leaped. The other was that I knew that I was sold to the English, and for fear of them, I did jump.... But I acted against my voices, and I was injured.... In leaping, I did not think to kill myself: I commended myself to God, and I thought in making that leap to escape." Painfully bruised but otherwise unhurt, she was returned to her cell, unable to eat or drink anything for several days; she was monitored by several guards who threatened to chain her by the neck to the wall if she repeated the deed.

During the subsequent weeks she was treated more rudely. One of the knights in Jean de Luxembourg's coterie, a Burgundian named Haimond de Macy, later admitted that he saw her "several times in prison, and on those occasions, I spoke with her. I also playfully tried, several times, to touch her chest and rub her breasts—but Joan would have none of it and repulsed me with a slap."

The negotiations for the sale of Joan were finally settled, and on December 6 Pierre Surreau, charged with finance ministry for Normandy, handed over the sum of ten thousand gold *écus* to a knight named Jean Bruyse, who in turn delivered to the duke of Luxembourg "the English money, on behalf of our king, in order to have Joan, called the Maid, who is now a prisoner of war." Precisely because she was a prisoner of war—and ennobled in the bargain—she should have been automatically protected by certain conventions to which aristocrats were loyal. But every one of those protections was ignored, and instead of being treated as a prisoner of war, she was treated as a dangerously irreligious person, a heretic, a living scandal. That was the only way to thoroughly disgrace her and her king; it would also be the short route to execution.

When Joan first visited Charles at Chinon in March 1429, the English controlled almost all of France north of the Loire River, including

Reims and Paris, and their victory at Orléans seemed assured. The heir
to the French throne, meanwhile, had no money, was badly advised,
and seemed destined never to be king. Fifteen months later, when Joan
was captured at Compiègne, Orléans had been saved for France, the
English had endured a number of crushing defeats, much of the occupied territory had been restored to Charles, and he had been crowned
at Reims.

It was therefore no exaggeration for anyone—historian, politician,
poet or peasant—to state that the girl from Domrémy had had an
impact on history so enormous that it alone might be called some kind
of miracle. She had friends and supporters everywhere in France—soldiers and townspeople, priests and aristocrats in all the places she had
visited and the regions she had saved for France. But they were helpless
against the wealth and power of dukes, princes and bishops.

At once the University of Paris sent a message to Henry VI: "We
have just learned that into your power is now delivered the woman
called the Maid—news at which we are entirely joyful, confident that
she will be brought to justice in order to redress the great wrongs and
scandals that have occurred here because of her." They hoped to hold
the trial in Paris, but Bedford realized that Paris was too politically mercurial, too near areas recently restored to Charles VII.

The trial should have been scheduled in the diocese where Joan was
captured—that is, the diocese of Beauvais; the regulations of a proper
Inquisition required that it be set either in the diocese of the prisoner's
birthplace or in the diocese where the alleged crimes were committed.
No one seriously considered moving the case as far as the marches of
Lorraine. As for Compiègne, that town lay in the diocese of Beauvais,
which had returned to Charles VII.

Normandy, by contrast, had long been an English fiefdom, and
Rouen was its capital. For sheer safety and prestige, that city was cho-
sen as the place for the trial; young Henry VI lived there with his tutor
Richard Beauchamp, Earl of Warwick. The decision to conduct the

trial in Rouen should have meant the immediate dismissal of Cauchon from the case, but the Duke of Bedford obviated that rule by granting Cauchon an extraterritorial authority for this case.

On Saturday, December 23, 1430, Joan arrived at Rouen and was imprisoned in a tower of Warwick's Bouvreuil castle, where he was to be her warden. Charged with heresy, she was denied all spiritual privileges and was not permitted to attend Mass on Christmas Day, which she spent shackled in an icy, dark chamber.

EIGHT

Cunning and Clothes

(January–February 1431)

Her tower cell was a dark, hexagonally shaped room just two meters wide, with a narrow window at one end and a latrine at the other. During the day Joan was rendered virtually immobile, chained to the wall by an iron band around her waist and her arms held by cuffs; at night additional shackles were attached to her ankles and then to a wooden block at the foot of a plank bed. She could not walk without assistance, nor was there any comfortable resting position. Cauchon guaranteed that she would not attempt another escape.

Five men in constant shifts kept watch over their prisoner, three of them remaining in the cell with her all night. "They were Englishmen of the lowest sort," according to Jean Massieu, the trial bailiff, or usher, who escorted Joan to and from the interrogations, "and they very much wanted her dead. They constantly mocked her, and she reprimanded them for their threats and insults." She was also on public display for strangers, who made her an object of rude curiosity at all hours.

Because she was nominally a Church convict to be tried by the Inquisition, Joan rightly complained that she should have been detained in an ecclesiastical keep, where she would have been guarded by women, and not in a military prison; her protests about this manifest violation of Inquisitorial procedure were ignored.

The threat of attack by her male guards was averted at least partly because of Joan's intricate attire, the laces and fastenings of the male garb she was permitted to retain only because it was planned as an important charge against her. Still, violent physical assault may have taken place were it not for the Duchess of Bedford, who visited Joan and then demanded that Warwick ban the guards from molesting their prisoner. "Still, some of the men tried to violate her," according to Guillaume Manchon, chief trial notary, "and if the Earl of Warwick had not run to her aid when she cried out for help, she would have been assaulted."

Joan was also menaced with a gruesome contraption. A tight cage was brought into the cell, and if her conduct warranted she would be forced to remain standing day and night in it, chained by the neck, hands, and feet to its bars. In his attempt to soften the impression of this dreadful situation and to suggest that Joan was indeed brought to a religious tribunal, Bishop Cauchon shared copies of the key to her cell with Henry Beaufort, cardinal of Winchester and the king's great-uncle, who was present at the trial, and with Jean d'Estivet, prosecutor of the Inquisition.

As the trial was being prepared, the irregularities accumulated. Not only was Joan improperly housed in a military prison and denied women as guards; it also became clear that all the expenses of the proceedings—court costs, compensation paid to judges, officers, assessors and clerks—were being borne by the English, who were in complete control of the case. Any semblance of fairness, therefore, was doomed at the outset. In addition, Joan had no advocate, and anyone who tried to counsel or to guide her was in jeopardy of censure or even grave punishments, on order of Cauchon. More to the point, Joan was denied access to a lawyer—a direct violation of the Church law stipulating that a person under twenty-five, accused of heresy, must have the defense of a seasoned lawyer. She was no more than nineteen.

• • •

TRIAL BY INQUISITION included two segments. First came the preparatory phase, a series of inquiries concerning allegations of guilt; at its conclusion the accused was either released or subjected to the next stage, a formal indictment. In Joan's case this opening segment began on January 9 and was completed on March 26. The second phase was the formal trial, during which the prisoner was confronted with articles of accusation and had to provide a defense; this was held from the end of March until May 24.

An Inquisition bore little resemblance to a secular court either then or later. First of all, only a rumor of shameful activity or heretical thinking was necessary to bring someone to trial. The task of the primary Inquisitor was that of the judge of the case: not to interrogate witnesses but to ascertain the thoughts and opinions of the one accused. Following Church law (which was based on Roman legal practice), those accused were presumed guilty and had to testify alone; they had no latitude to challenge witnesses and were denied the right of appeal. If convicted of heresy, a prisoner was turned over to secular authority and burned alive at the stake, a punishment that would prevent a magical escape and ensure that no relics would be left for veneration.

The preparatory phase of Joan's trial unofficially began in December 1430, when a team of court examiners, supervised by a notary named Nicolas Bailly, hurried to places where Joan was well known. They were commanded to find testimony or evidence against her—a futile effort since none could be found. No *diffamatio*, or scandalous allegation, could be logged against her, and Bailly reported that he had found nothing about the Maid that he would not have been happy to find about his own sister. With that it was clear that there were no grounds for a religious trial, and when Cauchon convened his court for the first time in January 1431, he had to ignore the negative results of his examiners' research.

In order to prove Joan a heretic, Cauchon would now have to inter-rogate her and try to catch her up in her own statements. She would have to confess to a serious crime, the nature of which was not to be disclosed to her or to the assembled assessors in advance. This was plainly illegal, for a heresy trial could not be based on the statements of the accused alone, nor could they be based on unspoken suspicions. But that was the procedure chosen in this case.

Cauchon's plans were further stymied in January when another physical examination, which Joan demanded, confirmed her virginity. With that, she could not be put on trial as a witch per se, although heresy was often considered a form of witchcraft. This was another set-back for Cauchon, who had hoped to demonstrate easily that Joan had misguided Charles VII by her contact with diabolical forces, that she was not in communion with God or the Church but rather with the powers of darkness—and that therefore the coronation of the king of France was null and void.

With the defamation and explicit witchcraft charges necessarily put aside, another approach was then taken: Joan's battle standard, Cauchon alleged, was under demonic control, and the rings she wore (gifts from her family and the king) were instruments of black magic; otherwise, why would common folk kneel to touch and kiss them? (Clearly, Cauchon saw no contradiction in his terms: everyone coming into his presence knelt and kissed his ring.) Furthermore, it was said that she fought cruelly; that she wore men's clothing in direct defiance of the book of Deuteronomy; and that she placed fidelity to her voices from God above her loyalty to the institutional Church. Taken collectively, Cauchon reasoned, those accusations ought to bring in a guilty verdict, and so he promised the Duke of Bedford.

As it happened, there was a significant, even a sublime, grain of truth in one accusation. Joan indeed claimed that her communication with God held a primacy in her life that superseded earthly authority. More than once she insisted that fidelity to God was paramount, of far greater importance than obedience to those who sought to interpret her experience. It seems never to have occurred to her—at least not until she was put on trial—that her experience of voices and visions would clash with the medieval requirement that spiritual experiences (especially those leading to heroic action) be submitted for Church adjudication.

THE COURT ASSEMBLED for Joan's trial had two judges: Pierre Cauchon, who successfully lobbied to be the director of the entire enterprise, and Jean Le Maître, the deputy Inquisitor for northern France. At first Le Maître rightly objected that Cauchon was not the proper judge because of his fiercely English bias and because he was not the presiding bishop of Rouen. A month after the trial began, Le Maître had yet to appear, and he was not seen until March 13, when he succumbed to Cauchon's pressure and did what he was told. "I see clearly," he confided to Jean Massieu, "that if I do not proceed as the English desire, I am looking at my own imminent death."

The chief prosecutor, Jean d'Estivet, a foul-mouthed brute despised even by Warwick, was quite frank in his hatred of Joan; thus Cauchon assured that d'Estivet was extremely prominent and influential during the trial, and Cauchon and d'Estivet put most of the questions to her. There were, as well, about sixty clergymen and theologians on the case; called assessors, or advisory consultants, they were selected because of their sympathies to England. Paid from an English purse, they were expected to be steadfast in their commitment to find Joan guilty.

The formal preliminaries of the trial, "in a matter of faith against a woman named Joan, commonly called the Maid," officially began on January 9, 1431. Eight assessors sat with Pierre Cauchon in the council chamber of Beauvreuil. The bishop then informed them that Joan "had recently been captured, and because she was suspected of being a heretic, had been handed over, at the request of the king of England

and the faculty of the University of Paris ... in order that inquiry might be made into the crimes and evil deeds of which she is accused, in order to give honor and praise to God and to exalt the holy Catholic faith."

Cauchon then distributed, for all to see, the letters testamentary from the clergy of Paris, of Rouen and of the court of England. He also read the names of those he had summoned, who had agreed to be assessors and clerks of the trial.

Manchon, the notary or chief note taker of the trial, later admitted, "I was compelled to serve, and I did so against my will—I wouldn't have dared to oppose the king's council. But the bishop of Beauvais [Cauchon] was not forced to act, nor was Jean d'Estivet. They acted quite freely and voluntarily. As for the assembled assessors, every single one of them was afraid of what would happen if they contradicted Cauchon and the English."

Massieu, who as usher accompanied Joan almost every day, found nothing but good in her, and when he expressed this opinion quite casually to someone in Warwick's household, his remark was reported. "That put me in a lot of trouble, but I got out of it by making excuses for myself."

A young theologian named Nicholas de Houppeville had also been forced into serving on the case. According to Massieu, "After seeing what was going on, he [Houppeville] had no desire to be involved—and so he was banished, along with a number of other dissenters." Before Houppeville was exiled, however, Cauchon made an example of him by tossing him into the Rouen prison, from which he was liberated only by the intervention of a kindly abbot. "As I saw it then and still see it today," he said twenty-five years later, "the trial was more of a deliberate persecution than a juridical process."

Such was also the opinion of Jean de Saint-Avit, the wise and just bishop of Avranches. He reminded Cauchon and the court that it was a custom hallowed since the thirteenth century (and the opinion of no less than Thomas Aquinas) that in such inflammatory and controversial matters as this trial, the case ought to be referred to the pope or to a general convocation of bishops. When he heard that, Cauchon simply dismissed Saint-Avit; but for his rank, Saint-Avit too might have faced imprisonment or exile on Cauchon's command.

Another assessor, a priest named Richard de Grouchet, later confessed that he (and others he named) "wanted to get out of the trial, but we finally took part out of fear and coercion." A priest named Jean Riquier summarized the process: "Everyone was either forced to please the English or did so voluntarily, and the English wanted a quick trial and a pretext to execute her."

A Dominican friar at Rouen named Isambart de la Pierre swore that he was threatened by Cauchon with death if he said anything good about Joan. The judges and assessors, according to la Pierre, were variously motivated by partisanship, outright hatred of Joan, love of the money with which they were bribed, or fear of punishment. "Everything was done according to the wishes of the King of England [that is, according to the mandate of his regent, the Duke of Bedford], the Cardinal of Winchester, the Earl of Warwick, and other Englishmen who assumed the trial's expenses."* As for Joan, a Benedictine monk named Thomas Marie summarized the *fama* or word of mouth in Rouen at the time: "If the English had a woman like Joan on their side, they would have rewarded her with high honors and not treated her so dreadfully."

That was also the judgment of Jean de la Fontaine, who was charged with making the summary of charges against Joan in February. He saw that the enormous evidence favorable to her was being deliberately excised from the record, and he promptly withdrew from the case; afraid for his life, he made a hasty exit from Rouen. Jean Lohier, a Norman priest, loudly proclaimed his opinion that the trial was invalid

---

* Many other testimonies support these; see, for example, the recollections of Martin Ladvenu, Jean Toutmouillé, Jean Le Fèvre, Jean Le Maire, Thomas Marie, Guillaume de la Chambre, and Jean de Mailly (the bishop of Noyon), all preserved in Duparc, *Procès en nullité*, vol. 1.

because no one was there to represent the cause of either Joan or Charles VII. "We shall ignore him and go on our way," muttered Cauchon. Lohier quit the trial and took refuge in Rome.

Cauchon's autocratic, tyrannical and malicious conduct with priests, bishops and assessors was entirely consistent with his attitude toward Joan, the trial he was preparing against her and his plan for her destruction. The critical issue at stake was clear to him: would Joan the Maid submit to the judgment of the institutional Church—that is, to him as its representative? Would she judge her own life as they would judge her? If so, she could readily be proclaimed guilty on their summary judgment; if she would not submit, she could nevertheless forthwith be condemned, since to deny the authority of the Church in matters spiritual was defined as the worst sort of heresy.

Cauchon's reasoning was a finely tuned example of medieval ecclesiastical thinking in service to churchmen rather than the laity; it was, in other words, an example of how a system could easily sacrifice people to syllogisms. However one assesses his sense of the Church, his notion of the nature of faith and the meaning of conscience, Cauchon can only be regarded as a complete failure; indeed, he gave no indication that these mattered to him at all. Entirely controlled by greed and an almost maniacal drive for political power, he became an implacable egomaniac who orchestrated not only Joan of Arc's condemnation as a heretic but also her death. He cannot simply be excused as a product of the fifteenth century, for people of that time—as seen in the reactions of many assessors—placed a high value on fidelity to canon and civil law, which he blithely ignored.

Utterly lacking any sense of justice, Cauchon insisted on stacking Joan's trial with biased minds. Then, to prove that he was fiercely loyal to the king of England and the English cause, he worked to destroy both the French throne and the woman who had brought its sovereign from the realm of the possible to the world of the real. His crime was among the most heinous, for he not only wished to demonstrate his intense loyalty to those who could raise him high, he also sought to destroy the perceived enemies of those he served. And if Joan the Maid was indeed an authentic visionary sent by God, he would have to consider himself doomed for supporting the wrong side in the Hundred Years' War. She had to be discredited, she had to be executed: his entire life, his success, his rank, reputation and position hung in the balance.

That Pierre Cauchon was a bishop with a keen mind intensified the awfulness of the situation. He revealed to the court nothing of Christian faith, much less of the spirit of the gospel or of the bishop's vocation—his mandate and, presumably, his sacred honor and supreme happiness—namely, the service of God's people. Of the man's earlier spiritual convictions, and of his conscience then and later, we know nothing.

THE FIRST PUBLIC session of the trial's preliminary investigation was held on Monday, February 19, when Cauchon in the presence of eleven assessors ordered Joan to make her first appearance two days later in council chambers. The next day Jean Le Maître informed Cauchon that he had no wish to be intimately involved in the trial or to appear on a regular basis, and he acquiesced in Cauchon's choice of d'Estivet as chief Inquisitorial promoter.

First Session: Ash Wednesday, February 21, 1431

On February 21 Joan of Arc first appeared at her own trial. She entered the council chamber, set up in the castle chapel, at eight o'clock that morning, escorted by Jean Massieu because the heavy chains on her hands, waist and feet made it impossible for her to walk without assistance. Joan had already been a prisoner, in one place or another, for almost nine months, and since before Christmas she had been denied the consolations of the Church's sacraments. That very morning she had asked to attend Mass before coming into the chamber, but Cauchon refused. Still, she had her own prayer and her communication with voices she still insisted came to her from God and His saints.

As she looked around the room, Joan saw more than three dozen theologians, doctors of canon and civil law, judges and clerks. Cauchon, convinced that he could make short work of an illiterate peasant girl who had risen beyond her station, wasted no time as he and d'Estivet alternated asking the first questions:

Questioner: To shorten this trial and to unburden your conscience, you must swear on this book of the Holy Gospels to tell the whole truth concerning everything that will be asked of you.

Joan: I do not know what you want to question me about. Perhaps you may ask about private things, which I will not answer.

The "private things" referred not only to the intimacy of her spiritual life and the nature of her visions and voices, but also to whatever she knew of French military plans, strategies and matters past and present relative to the king of France. Of these things, she always refused to speak; hence she would not take an oath to answer truthfully everything put to her:

Joan: I am ready to swear to tell the truth concerning what I know about this trial—but I shall never say everything that I know.

Questioner: You must swear to tell the truth about whatever you are asked that relates to the Catholic faith—and anything else that you may know.

Joan: I shall willingly swear to tell you everything about my father and mother, and what I have done since I came into France [that is, the part of the country loyal to Charles VII]. But I have never said anything to anyone about the revelations I have been given by God—except to Charles, who is my earthly king. And even if you threaten to cut my head off, I will not reveal anything, for God asks me to keep these revelations secret.

Questioner: Swear to tell the truth concerning your faith.

Joan took the missal in her hands and swore to speak truthfully in all matters concerning the faith. She then added, "But about my revelations, I will tell you nothing." She was then required to begin with a traditional and formal statement that revealed her name, origins and background.

Joan: I was born in Domrémy de Greux, and the principal church of the region is at Greux. In that place, I was called Jeannette, and in France, Jeanne [= Joan]. My father is Jacques Darc, and my mother is Isabelle.

Questioner: Where were you baptized?

Joan: In the church of Domrémy.

Questioner: Who were your godmothers and godfathers?

Joan: They were women called Agnes and Jeanne, and a man named Jean Bavent. My mother told me there were other godmothers and godfathers too.

Questioner: Which priest baptized you?

Joan: His name was Jean Minet, so far as I can recall.

Questioner: Is he still alive?

Joan: I think so.

Questioner: How old are you?

Joan: About nineteen.

Questioner: Who gave you religious instruction?

Joan: My mother taught me the Our Father and the Hail Mary and the Apostles' Creed. No one but my mother taught me about faith.

Questioner: Say the Lord's Prayer and the Ave María aloud.

    Joan: If you hear my confession, I will gladly do so.

This was a clever request on Joan's part, for it could never be denied by any priest. But this would have required Cauchon to shift roles, from judge to priestly confessor, and he would have had to accord her forgiveness. According to Church law, it also would have prevented him from revealing in public anything she told him within the seal of confession. Cauchon said he would provide another clergyman among those present to hear her confession, but she refused to say prayers aloud, as he requested, unless Cauchon himself heard her. He dropped the subject. She then complained about her shackles.

Questioner: Several times you have tried to escape from your prisons, so to keep you more securely, I have ordered that you be shackled.

    Joan: Of course I tried to escape—that is to be expected of any prisoner! And if I had been able to escape, no one could accuse me of breaking my word, for I would never give any-one my word that I would not try.

Hearing that, Cauchon ordered the chief of Joan's guards to keep strict watch over her at all times, to see that her chains were secure at all hours, and not to allow anyone to visit or speak with her unless they had his own explicit permission.

At that point, and with Cauchon's approving glance, several assessors spoke simultaneously, crying out questions and making statements to Joan in an attempt to confuse and intimidate her. "When the Lord of Beauvais and six assessors first interrogated her," recalled Jean Massieu, "it was usual for one to ask her a question, and while she was answering, another interrupted her reply with another question, so that she had to call out for some order in the hall."

Joan: My lord and my lords, I beg you—one question at a time, please, and I shall reply!

Displeased by her poise, Cauchon adjourned the session.

Guillaume Manchon, the chief notary or recorder of the trial, later testified as to the general tone of the proceedings:

During the trial, she was often exhausted by the many repeated and complicated questions, which were sometimes put to her simultaneously. They put her through this every morning for three or four hours, and often late in the day too for another two or three hours. Many times they quoted her to herself from a previous day's record, even changing her words in order to confuse her. Despite this, she spoke firmly and clearly, for she had a superb memory. Often she said, in response to a question, "I already replied to that," and if they said she had not, she said, "I refer you to the master notary," meaning myself, who was the recorder of her words. She was always correct in her memory of what she had said.

At the beginning there was often a great deal of confusion and disarray in the chapel turned judicial chamber. In addition to Manchon, the English had imported their own secretaries, who frequently shouted aloud for Joan or one of the assessors to repeat something while she was replying. With considerable courage, Manchon announced that he would no longer continue in his assigned task if this sort of chaos continued. Soon after, the trial was moved to a small court of the castle. Years later Manchon said:

I set down the Maid's answers in French, and sometimes the judges tried to force me to put those answers in other words—for they referred to them in Latin and changed the meaning of her words or my taking of dictation. Meanwhile, Cauchon had other secretaries taking down Joan's answers and changing them. My notes were put in the minutes, as required, but [Cauchon] often referred to the notes of others when he was questioning Joan.

Second Session: Thursday, February 22

The second day the trial was moved to the *chambre de parement*, a small room adjacent to the Great Hall of the castle. A Rouen priest named Jean Beaupère, one of the assessors, asked the questions, which dealt mostly with Joan's voices and the events of Vaucouleurs. At the outset Joan was again asked to take the oath swearing to answer about everything she would be asked.

> *Joan:* I gave you that oath yesterday. You are burdening me too much. I will tell the truth concerning any points touching the faith, but that is all.

This was not mere stubbornness on Joan's part. She knew they were trying to convict her of heresy—errors in her beliefs—and she was confident that she could acquit herself in that regard. She also knew that there were biblical and canonical prohibitions against needless oath taking—and it was not beyond possibility that her judges, having asked her to take repeated oaths, would omit their requests from the transcripts, include only her multiple oaths, and then condemn her for having taken them.

> *Questioner:* Will you tell us the truth about everything?
> *Joan:* If you really knew me, about my life and what I have done, you would really want to have nothing to do with me, and you would know that you have no reason to charge or condemn me. I have done nothing except by revelation from God.

Typically, the interrogation shifts in subject and chronology.

Questioner: How old were you when you left home?

    Joan: I am not sure.

Questioner: Did you learn any craft or trade?

    Joan: My mother taught me very well how to sew, and I don't think there's a woman here in Rouen who could teach me anything more about it.

Questioner: Why did you leave Domrémy with your family?

    Joan: For fear of the Burgundians. We stayed with a woman at Neufchâteau, and there I helped with household tasks.

Questioner: Did you go to confession every year? [Annual confession was required by Church law.]

    Joan: Yes, to my own parish priest, and if he was not available, then to another. I also went to confession to friars who visited the town. And I went to Holy Communion every year at Easter [as also required by Church law].

Questioner: Did you go to Holy Communion at other feasts than Easter?

This too was a trick question. If she said she did, then they would have inquired about the state of her soul each time she did so, to whom she confessed and so forth. And if she did not frequent the Eucharist outside Eastertide, they were free to ask why not since this could have been interpreted as an implication of sinfulness. Hence her reply:

    Joan: Go to the next question.

Questioner: We understand that you claim to have heard voices. When did you first hear voices?

    Joan: At about the age of thirteen, I heard a voice from Our Lord, teaching me how to behave. The first time I was very much afraid. It happened about noon on a summer day, when I was in my father's garden, and I heard the voice on my right side, as if from the direction of the church. There was also a bright light—I always saw a bright light, and it was always in the direction of the voice. The voice always took good care of me, and I felt very consoled.

Questioner: What sort of teaching did the voice give you?

Joan: I was taught how to behave, to pray, and to go to church. Later I was told go to into France. Later still, two or three times a week, I was told I must leave home and go to raise the siege of Orléans—but first I must go to Robert de Baudricourt, the captain of Vaucouleurs, and that he would give me men to accompany me. Twice Baudricourt refused me, but then he received me and gave me men to conduct me to France.... Before that, the Duke of Lorraine sent for me. I went with safe conduct and told him I could do nothing for his health but that I would pray for him.

Questioner: Who advised you to put on men's clothing?

Joan: My voices ... but I charge no one with this.

Joan answered variously to this question, but there are no real discrepancies. She repeatedly said that she was inspired to wear male garb for the obvious practical reasons and for protection against both military and sexual danger. And when she replied that no one told her to do so, she simply meant that the notion came from no outside agent or command. She then described how she left Vaucouleurs and who accompanied her, and she told of their journey to Charles.

Joan: I found my king at Chinon, where I arrived about noon and went to an inn. Then I went to where the king was, and I recognized him. I told the king that I wished to do battle against the English.

The questions then shifted to the frequency of her voices during her interviews with the king, about which Joan said very little. They asked about her injury during the siege of Paris, who cared for her and various other matters—all designed to confuse her by mixing the chronology. By late afternoon Cauchon was hungry and concluded the day's proceedings, calling for a day's recess.

Third Session: Saturday, February 24

The trial reconvened on Saturday with a long speech by Cauchon reminding her that he was her judge and that she was required to do his bidding in all things.

> *Joan:* Beware of saying that you are my judge. In so doing, you
> take upon yourself a very great responsibility, and you place
> too great a burden on me. My lord bishop, I have come
> from God, and I ought not to be here before you. You
> should dismiss me and place me in the hands of God, from
> whom I came.

Beaupère then resumed the inquiry:

Questioner: When did you last eat or drink?
> *Joan:* Yesterday afternoon.
Questioner: When did you last hear your voices?
> *Joan:* Yesterday and today.
Questioner: At what time?
> *Joan:* Yesterday, three times—in the morning, at the hour of
> Vespers [late afternoon] and at the hour of the Ave Maria
> [at six in the evening].

Questioner: What were you doing when you heard this voice?*

    Joan: I was asleep, and the voice awoke me.

Questioner: How were you awakened—by the sound of the voice, or
              did someone touch you on the arm, or elsewhere?

    Joan: By the voice, without being touched.

Cauchon never admitted that Joan was confined to a cell:

Questioner: Is the voice still in your room?

    Joan: I think not, but perhaps somewhere in the castle....

Questioner: What did the voice tell you?

    Joan: To ask for counsel and assistance from Our Lord.

Questioner: Is it the voice of an angel or a saint?

Joan's reply was shrewd:

    Joan: The voice came from God. And a light comes before the
            voice.

Then, as if inspired at that same moment, she said to Cauchon:

    Joan: You say that you are my judge. Take care about what you are
            doing, for indeed, I have been sent by God, and you are put-
            ting yourself in great spiritual danger.... And as for me, I
            know that people are sometimes hanged for telling the truth.

Then followed one of the most famous exchanges, preserved identi-
cally in all manuscript sources and much repeated in literary works
about her through the centuries:

---

* Both Joan and her judges alternate between the singular and plural use of *voice*,
which, on her side, is to be expected of any attempt to put a mystical experience into
ordinary language.

Questioner: Do you consider yourself in a state of grace?

This was a question with hooks. It meant, "Do you consider yourself in God's favor?" If Joan answered yes, she would be accused at once of presumption and condemned as a heretic, since it was taught that no person can be certain of his own spiritual condition. But if Joan replied no, she would be admitting that she was in serious sin and she would be condemned on the spot. And so she spoke her profound and canny answer, which dealt with every angle of the challenge:

> *Joan:* If I am not in the state of grace, may God put me there—
> and if I am, may He keep me there.

The court, according to the notary Boisguillaume, was *multum stupefacti,* "much astonished," at the wisdom of her reply. Hence Cauchon at once changed the subject, trying to throw Joan off course.

Questioner: In your childhood, did the voice tell you to hate the
Burgundians?
Joan: The Burgundians will always have war if they do not do as
they ought to do; this I know from my voices.
Questioner: In your childhood, did the voices tell you that the English
would come into France?
Joan: They were already here when they first spoke to me!
Questioner: When you were young, did you have a great desire to fight
the Burgundians?

Her reply dealt neatly with that provocation:

> *Joan:* I had a great desire that our king should have his
> kingdom.

The judges then encouraged Joan to admit to some kind of witch-craft or at least a belief in it. In a meadow near Domrémy was a beauti-ful tree, sometimes called the Fairy Tree by children who played there in the summer and by engaged couples and families who often ate pic-nic lunches in the cool shade under its ample branches.

Questioner: Isn't it true that there was a spring near the tree, where people suffering from fever took a drink and were cured?

Joan: I heard about that, but I do not know if it is true. The tree itself was a large beech tree, and some of the girls hung gar-lands on its branches. But as soon as I learned that I must come to the aid of the dauphin, I played very little—the least I could.

Questioner: Is there not a prophecy that says that a girl would come from a forest near your home and perform wonderful acts?

Joan: I put no faith in that sort of thing.

Questioner: Do you want to wear a woman's dress?

Joan: If you give me one, I will take it and go. Otherwise, I am content with what I am wearing, since it is God's will that I wear it.

The issue of Joan wearing male clothing was of supreme importance to Pierre Cauchon, who finally prepared his case with this as the single issue charged against her. It was a specious matter, of course.

The twenty-second chapter of the book of Deuteronomy, invoked as the sanction against her male garments, prohibited cross-dressing: "A woman shall not wear a man's apparel, nor shall a man put on a wom-an's garment, for whoever does such things is abhorrent to the Lord your God." This was proscribed in ancient times in order to prevent the Israelites from imitating or being associated with the cultic rites of their pagan neighbors, who worshipped the Mesopotamian goddess

Ishtar in wild sexual rites that were characterized by transvestism and orgies.

But any reading of the ancient legal restrictions in Deuteronomy that tries to impose them on every subsequent era of history is bound to trip on itself. The same chapter of that book also prescribes that clothes may not be made of a combination of wool and linen; that adultery is to be punished by instant execution; and that a disobedient and intemperate son is to be stoned to death. Israelite law itself modified and even abrogated many of the sanctions set in ancient contexts that were no longer applicable. The genius of the later rabbinic movement was in fact the belief that laws, cultic practices and moral restrictions must take into account the continuing presence and revelation of God to His people. In any case, Cauchon was fishing, and in the matter of Joan's male attire he claimed more and more to have caught something big.

More to the point, medieval moral theologians always permitted cross-dressing for good reasons, as no less an authority than Thomas Aquinas observed in the thirteenth century: "Apparel should be consistent with the estate of the person, according to the general custom. For a woman to wear a man's clothes, or vice versa ... is expressly forbidden in the Law because the Gentiles used to practice this change of attire for the purpose of idolatrous superstition. Nevertheless this may be done sometimes on account of some necessity, either in order to hide oneself from enemies, or through lack of other clothes, or for some similar motive."

Even before Aquinas, another influential remark on the subject was made by Hildegard of Bingen in the twelfth century: "A man should never put on feminine dress, or a woman male attire, unless a man's life or a woman's chastity is in danger; at such times, a man may change his clothes for a woman's, and a woman for a man's." Indeed, the Church routinely permitted cross-dressing for purposes of safety: Bedford's own sister-in-law disguised herself as a soldier in order to escape from Philip of Burgundy. She was not put on trial for heresy.

Manchon testified to the practical reasons for Joan's insistence on wearing male garb in prison:

> She repeatedly said she needed it, for at night her guards tried to violate her ... [and] it was only the tightly laced pants that discouraged her jailers. At least once, that almost happened, when she cried out and the Earl [Warwick] himself ran to her aid—if he had not, she would have been assaulted.... She was not safe in a woman's garb among those guards, [and] she insisted that if her judges would consign her to a safe place [a Church prison, where she would be guarded by nuns], where she would not have to fear attack, then she would gladly put on a woman's dress.

In fact, Joan had her defenders in this matter even during her lifetime. At the time of her victory at Orléans, the theologian Jean Gerson indicated that her military situation indeed required her to wear male garb; and Jacques Gelu, the archbishop of Embrun, remarked that such apparel was fitting. Sometimes theologians display remarkable common sense.

Fourth Session: Tuesday, February 27

Jean Beaupère opened the following Tuesday with ostensible benignity:

Questioner: How have you been since last Saturday?
    Joan: As well as I can be, given my circumstances.

In this reply we hear both her calm humility and her refusal either to seek pity or to dramatize the dreadfulness of her condition. In addition to the physical pain of her confinement, the constant terror of attack, and the injuries to her skin and joints from the chains, she was deprived of light and air, denied the rituals of her faith, mocked, threatened, and given just enough meager food and drink to survive. The once-daily meal handed to an imprisoned heretic normally consisted of a bowl of water (sometimes mixed with ashes as a symbol of penance) and a bit of thin soup or a few animal bones—something left over from the lavish plates of the judges' meals.

In response to further questions, Joan then identified her voices.

> *Joan:* I have told you often enough about them. Believe me if you will.
>
> *Questioner:* Was there an angel over your king's head when you first saw him?
>
> *Joan:* If there were any, I did not know, nor did I see one.

Pressed to repeat earlier information, she then told again of her first meeting with the king, her journey to Poitiers, and her outfitting for battle. The notaries observed her pallor, and there may have been some apprehension that Joan would faint. To forestall the sympathy that might evoke from some of those present, Cauchon ended the session.

NINE

A Dress for a Mass

(March 1431)

The trial resumed the following Thursday.

Fifth Trial Session: Thursday, March 1

Cauchon began by asking Joan yet again to take an oath that she would answer every question; again, she refused—and, rightly following Jewish and Christian custom, she said that multiple oaths were both unnecessary and offensive.

An important matter arose early that day:

Questioner: Did you usually have the names of Jesus and Mary, with a cross, placed on the letters you dictated?

Joan: On some I put them, and on others not. I put a cross as a sign that anyone who was French to whom I was writing should not believe the contents or do as I asked in the letter.

The cross, then, was a code: a letter with a cross, if intercepted by an enemy, would deliberately contain false and deceptive information; if sent to an ally aware of the code, the letter was simply not believed. Joan was then asked her opinions about the earlier claims of three men to the papacy during the Great Schism.

> *Joan:* I never wrote or dictated anything concerning the three popes, and I will swear to that.

There followed a lengthy exchange during which Cauchon tried to reduce Joan's visions and voices to the level of absurdity.

> *Questioner:* Do your saints always wear the same dress?... What part of them do you see?... Do they have hair?... Is their hair worn long?... Do they have arms and legs?... What language do they speak?

The judges clearly hoped that Joan would be too descriptive, too literal in her details, thus turning her visions and voices into either illusions or idols; again, they were disappointed:

> *Joan:* I know nothing of their clothing.... I see their faces.... Of their hair or their arms I can say nothing.... Of their language, why should they speak English? They are not on the side of the English!
>
> *Questioner:* Does Saint Michael appear naked?
>
> *Joan:* Don't you think that Our Lord has the ability to clothe him?

The judges then interrogated Joan concerning details of the court of Charles VII, his plans, his strategies, his faith. To everything asked of her about her king, Joan's reply was invariable:

> *Joan:* You will not drag any of that out of me. I have told you earlier that I have nothing to say about the king.

It seemed preposterous to this court that an uneducated young woman would speak with such blunt confidence. The trial was becoming a match of wits; it was also a contest of pure faith against an institution.

But on its deepest level, this was also a trial concerning the absolute freedom of God Himself. Against that freedom, it is always tempting to maintain that God will certainly act in such-and-such a way; that a Church must be structured in such-and-such a way, with an essential male power elite and a clear line of command that guarantees the survival of orthodoxy. This has always been the most dangerous presumption of organized religion: ignoring the centrality of God while slavishly preserving a merely human representation or expression of Him. But God does not conform to human presumptions, nor is His freedom limited. There is no reason why God cannot summon an illiterate provincial girl to a task we would see better suited for a trained general. There is no reason why God must conform to the lowest common denominator of human expectation.

Sixth Session: Saturday, March 3

During the following session two days later, Jean Beaupère tried to goad Joan into speaking impatiently and inaccurately, contradicting herself on the matter of her voices; this he did by repeated questions about the wings, arms and legs of the figures in her visions. This brief exchange is typical of the entire morning interrogation:

Questioner: Do you believe that God made your saints with heads just as you see them?

Joan: I saw them with my own eyes; that is all I will say.

Questioner: Do your voices tell you that you will escape?

Joan: I place everything in the hands of Our Lord, who will do as he pleases.

It was becoming clear to Cauchon's court that there was no foundation for charges of witchcraft, sorcery, magic or immorality. And so the
bishop began to exploit his unequivocal prohibition against wearing
male garb and to link this to the issue of submission to the Church
(that is, to him). It was a resourceful but astonishingly arrogant move.
By wearing pants, it was charged, Joan had riven the firm line separating women from male status and prerogatives. Her clothing, her deeds
in battle, her skill in dealing with princes, knights, soldiers and common folk—all this was seen as proper to men, and for her to claim
male prerogatives was (to Cauchon) abominable.

At the same time, Joan set up her own spiritual experience as her
primary authority even if it was challenged by mere institutional command. She was therefore defying male supremacy by wearing men's
clothes and entering into the world of men as a woman who considered
her communication with God inviolable.

Questioner: Do you believe you would do wrong in taking a woman's
dress?
Joan: It is better to obey my sovereign Lord God rather than
men.

Her words went to the heart of the trial. For Joan, the will of
Cauchon or the court or indeed any man was superseded by her experience of God, by her conviction about the will of God for her. It was better to refer to God than to men.

Joan: I know for certain that my God has always been the master
of my actions, that I have never done anything but what I
knew to be His will for me, and that no evil spirit has had
any control over me. My words and deeds have been and
are always in the hands of God.

A recess was declared, after which Cauchon continued:

Questioner: Do you know whether your countrymen [those loyal to
Charles VII] firmly believe that you were sent by God?
Joan: I don't know if they believe that—but even if they do not
believe it, I am still sent by God.
Questioner: If they do believe it, are they right?
Joan: If they believe that I am sent by God, they are not wrong.

Trying to level a charge of idolatry, or at least pride, he asked:

Questioner: What about the people who came to you, kissing your
hands and clothing and feet?
Joan: Many people came to see me, and I always tried to prevent
such gestures from them. But the poor often came to me
because I was kind to them and did as much as I could for
them.

DURING THE FOLLOWING week Cauchon and the assessors began to
compile a list of articles against Joan. Before they could complete that
task, however, they had to put further questions to her. At the same time
Cauchon ordered that all future interrogations would be conducted only
by himself and a few colleagues and that they would be held not in an
open court but in Joan's cell. She would remain bound and isolated but
for their visits, which became increasingly menacing.

A process of additional psychological torture was now designed to
eradicate her confidence while further restricting her mobility: at each
moment, she would be in the physical position of a chained supplicant.
And only Cauchon and his handpicked cronies were there to hear her
brave and prudent replies and rejoinders; even the notaries were now
working at Cauchon's nod.

His stratagem had the desired effect. Joan was soon worn down, confused and exhausted; although she remained adamant on the essential points of her life, her work, and her visions, she was no longer the calm and confident girl of the open court. Her replies were now frequently vague, often contradictory, sometimes extravagant—as if she was giving Cauchon what he wanted, to have done with him. Malnourishment, lack of sleep, constant anxiety and physical confinement were taking a dreadful toll on her stamina.

Seventh Session: Saturday, March 10

At the next session a week later, after answering questions about the battle at Compiègne, about her coat of arms and her conduct in battle, Joan did not help herself by making an ingenuous remark:

> Joan: I always thanked Our Lord for freeing me from the trouble caused by some clergymen in France, who argued against me. I prayed very much about that.

Eighth Session: Monday Morning, March 12

> Questioner: We are commanded to honor our fathers and mothers. Do you think it was right to leave home without your parents' permission?
>
> Joan: In everything else, all my life, I was obedient to them, except for my departure. But later I wrote to them, and they forgave me this incident.
>
> Questioner: So when you left them, you committed a sin!
>
> Joan: What I did is what God had commanded, and so I had to obey. If I had a hundred fathers and mothers and if I had been the daughter of a king, I would still have gone.

There followed one of the most important moments of Joan's trial, in which she spoke a basic tenet of universal spirituality:

Questioner: Do your voices and spirits stay with you for a long time?
Joan: They often come to Christians who do not see them, and I have often been aware of them among Christian folk.

It is axiomatic that God does not play favorites. Joan of Arc is only one among many, one of the celebrated in history among those who made an enormous impact on the world and whose actions were predicated on an experience of God. Every true mystic, everyone who has known a fleeting experience of the eternal, knows that this world is interpenetrated with that of the spirit. God is not distant; those who have died are in God and are therefore not distant. The world of angels, spirits and saints is but one sort of hierophantic language to describe the real presence of another world, beyond but in the midst of our own.

This is not to speak of necromancy or bogus spiritualism; it is to affirm that everything in the world belongs to God, who manifests Himself in and through creation but is neither defined nor limited by it. "Voices and spirits often come to Christians who do not see them." That is a wise indictment of spiritual torpor, a failure to "hear" and to "see" the truth that, as Gerard Manley Hopkins wrote, "The world is charged with the grandeur of God."

Ninth Session: Monday Afternoon, March 12

At the following session Cauchon was absent, likely meeting with Le Maître on the formal articles of condemnation. Hence Beaupère came to Joan's cell with four clerics, who conducted repetitious interrogations concerning Joan's obedience to her parents and her use of male garb.

Tenth Session: Tuesday, March 13

The following day, asked about the vision of the crown of the king of France, which she had said was brought to Charles by an angel when she was at Chinon, she gave an elaborate account—highly stylized, as if from a storybook. Typical of the language of her time, Joan's description was a kind of parable about the dramatic divine intervention that came to Charles with her arrival, and the fulfillment of her mission when he was crowned at Reims.

Eleventh Session: Wednesday Morning, March 14

Questioner: Why did you leap from the tower at Beaurevoir?

Joan: I heard that the people of Compiègne were to be put to death, and I would rather have died than live after such a catastrophe. Another reason was that I knew I had been sold to the English, and death was preferable than falling into their hands.

Questioner: Did your voices advise you to jump?

Joan: Saint Catherine told me almost every day not to do it, and that God would help both me and the people of Compiègne. And I told Saint Catherine that since God was going to help those people, I wanted to be there. She told me to take all this in good grace, that I would not be freed until I saw the English king. I replied that I did not wish to see him and that I would rather die than fall into the hands of the English.

Questioner: Did you intend to kill yourself?

Joan: No, but when I did it, I put myself in God's hands and really thought that if I jumped I would escape and avoid being turned over to the English.

Questioner: According to your earlier remarks, after your recovery from the fall you denied and cursed God and His saints.

Joan: I never denied or cursed God or His saints—then or at any other time.... I have asked only three things of my voices: that I should be freed; that God would help the French and safeguard the towns in their jurisdiction; and that I would save my own soul.... I do not know if I will be delivered from prison or not, but my voices have told me, "Take it all in a good spirit, and do not despair on account of your martyrdom, for you will finally come to the kingdom of heaven." My voices told me this firmly and simply. And I knew that my martyrdom is the pain and suffering I am undergoing here in prison. I do not know if there will be more to suffer, but I put all my faith in Our Lord.

Questioner: Do you mean to claim that you are certain of salvation and that you will not be damned?

Joan: I firmly believe what my voices have told me—that I will be saved—and I know it as firmly as if I were already there.

Questioner: Well, then, do you believe that you cannot commit serious sin?

Joan: I know nothing of that, but I commit myself in all things to God.

"In her manner, she was very simple and straightforward," recalled Friar Martin Ladvenu, "but her answers were full of common sense and insight."

Twelfth Session: Wednesday Afternoon, March 14

That afternoon Joan asked to clarify her final response of the morning:

> Joan: I know that I cannot commit sin if I keep the vow and promise I made to Our Lord, that I will keep my virginity of body and soul.

> Questioner: Since you are so certain of being saved, do you think you must confess serious sin?

> Joan: I do not know that I have committed any serious sin, but I believe that Saint Catherine and Saint Margaret would abandon me if I did.

> Questioner: Do you not believe that taking a man prisoner, keeping him for ransom, and then executing him is a mortal sin?

> Joan: I have never done anything like that.

> Questioner: What about the man Franquet d'Arras [a notorious war criminal]?

> Joan: He was a murderer, a thief, and a traitor, and I agreed with the sentence of execution, But his trial lasted two weeks ... and I sought to have him exchanged for the Seigneur de l'Ours in Paris. When I learned that he was dead, I said that Franquet d'Arras should be dealt with as justice required....

Then a list of charges was read: that she had attacked Paris on a religious holiday; that she had stolen a bishop's horse; that she had thrown herself down from the tower at Beaurevoir; that she had worn and was still wearing male garb; that she agreed to the death of d'Arras. Taken together:

> Questioner: Do you not believe yourself to be in a state of grave sin?

> Joan: I do not believe so—and if I am, it is for God to know it, and for the priest who hears me in confession.

DESPITE HER INTENSE, unremitting suffering and the psychological strain placed on her, nineteen-year-old Joan of Arc remained remarkably poised and unwavering in the conviction of the state of her soul and the reality of the consolation she received from God.

At this point it is tempting to imagine that spiritual solace must have canceled her emotional struggle and diminished the effects of her physical agony, but this was not the case. The literature on the topic, from autobiographical accounts to careful studies of lives ancient and modern, reveals that, however we understand it and however intense it may be, a relationship with God does not remove the mystery of suffering. One has only to consider a few obvious examples—the suffering of Jeremiah, the agony of Jesus, the struggles of Buddha, the dark nights of the saints: an experience of God's nearness does not mean an avoidance of pain; it does, however, provide a path through which suffering may be endured.

The meaning of suffering for an individual and the reason for the existence of evil in the world may never be satisfactorily explained by philosophers or theologians. But faith provides, for lack of a better term, a coping mechanism: we may trust absolutely that nothing is lost to God, that He knows, embraces and ultimately transforms suffering.

Is it more comforting to assert the ultimate meaninglessness of life? Is nihilism more consoling than clinging to God in faith, saying, "I do not know, I do not see—but I trust in You, my God"? Does denial of meaning, even when we cannot know it, bring peace and diminish agony? "No matter how deep our darkness, God is deeper still," Corrie ten Boom wrote from the unimaginable suffering of a Nazi death camp. She was right: God does not preserve us *from* all suffering, but He does preserve us *in* all suffering.

A century before Joan, Julian of Norwich put the matter another way: "God did not say, 'You will not be tempted, you will not be belabored, you will not be disquieted, you will not suffer'—but He did say, 'You shall not be overcome.'" That kind of conviction lay at the root of Joan's faith, enabling her to withstand the gathering storm that rendered her inactive and powerless. In that regard as in others, she takes

her place with the great souls whose faith, even in the deepest darkness, must leave us mute with admiration.

JOAN WAS COMPELLED to reply to the list of charges. As for the
bishop's horse:

> *Joan:* It was sent back to the bishop as soon as I learned he was dis-
> pleased—and in any case, the horse was useless for riding.

About her leap from the tower:

> *Joan:* I did not do it out of despair but to save my life from the
> English and to go to the aid of the people of Compiègne.
> Yes, it was wrong of me to make that jump, and I confessed
> it later.
> *Questioner:* Were you given a heavy penance for your sin?
> *Joan:* The pain of recovery was penance enough.
> *Questioner:* Do you not think that jumping was a mortal sin?
> *Joan:* I do not know—I place myself in Our Lord's hands.

And when she was asked again about her male clothes:

> *Joan:* I wear these clothes at the command of God and in His ser-
> vice, so I cannot believe that I do wrong. When it pleases
> Him to order me, I shall put them aside.

Thirteenth Session: Thursday Morning , March 15

Cauchon had devised a subtle argument by which he expected Joan to
condemn herself. If she had said or done anything contrary to the faith

of the Church, he asked her, would she not submit to the Church's judgment of her and correct herself or be corrected? If Joan said she would submit, then everything—her voices and visions, her words and deeds—could be proclaimed sinful. If she would not submit, the outcome was self-evident.

> Joan: I would like my testimony to be examined and studied by priests and scholars, who will tell me if I have done anything contrary to Christian faith. Then I will consult my voices, and if there is anything against the faith, I would not uphold it but would abandon that position at once.

This seems a contradictory response, but it makes solid sense: Joan says, essentially, "Show me what is unorthodox, and I will confer with my voices, but of course I have no wish to be a heretic." She maintains a fine balance between intellectual humility and confidence that she has not been led astray; she maintains that there can be no contradiction between the command of God to her and the requirements of faith.

She was then given a brief lecture on one of the favorite themes of medieval piety, the distinction between the Church Triumphant and the Church Militant. The former term refers to all those who have gone before and are in the glory of heaven with the risen Christ; the latter means the faithful here and now, struggling against sin and evil—and led, it was believed, by the wisdom and holiness of the pope, cardinals, bishops, and clergy. Joan had to submit, she was told, to the judgment of the Church Militant with regard to her claims.

The argument must have confused her, for she simply replied, "I will not give you any answer right now." With that, the court announced a recess.

"They convened long hours of interrogation," according to Jean Fabri, a bishop and scholar who was present.

She was always articulate and prudent, no matter how they tired her out. And to everyone's amazement, she interrupted a notary if he read something incorrect from the record. Once, Manchon went back to consult his notes and he had to admit that Joan was right. He promised he would be more accurate thereafter, and Joan playfully replied that if he made a mistake again, she would pull his ears for him!

Fourteenth Session: Thursday Afternoon, March 15

Questioner: Do you believe that God would permit you to escape from prison if you could?

Joan: I would gladly try to escape from any prison. If I saw a door open, I would go, for that would mean God's permission— "Help yourself and God will help you!"

Questioner: You have asked to attend Mass. Don't you think it would be more appropriate to wear a woman's dress to Mass? What would you prefer: to wear a dress and go to Mass or keep your man's clothing and not hear Mass?

Joan: Promise me that I may go to Mass if I wear a dress, and I will answer you that.

Questioner: Yes, I promise you.

Joan: But suppose I have promised God not to take off these garments? Well, make me a long dress for Mass, and after that, I will put these clothes back on.

Questioner: No, you must wear woman's clothing, without condition or limitation and forever.

Joan: I will do that to go to Mass.

There was a brief pause, and then Joan (perhaps thinking of the danger of changing and of wearing less protective clothing) changed her mind:

Joan: I beg you to allow me to keep the clothes I have and go to Mass.

Questioner: Will you not submit this and everything else to the judgment of the Church?

Joan: Everything I have said and done is in God's hands, and I commit myself to Him alone. I assure you that I would not say or do anything against Christian faith.

Questioner: Will you submit to Church law?

Joan: I will say nothing further now. But send me a clerk this Saturday, and what I have to say will be put down in writing.

Evidently Joan was exhausted at this point, but Cauchon, Beaupère and Le Maître badgered her with further repetitious inquiries about the appearance of the saints and angels in her visions, about the counsel they gave her in battle and about her escape attempts. Finally, she had had enough:

Joan: I have told you all of this. Look at the record of the last days and you will have your answers.

Fifteenth Session: Saturday Morning, March 17

The interrogations on Saturday continued in Joan's cell, with ever fewer judges and notaries. Cauchon was present, but the questions were asked by others, who also had to take down notes. Also present were Jean Massieu and Isambart de la Pierre.

Questioner: Will you submit all your words and actions to the judgment of the Church?

Joan: I love the Church and will support it with all my might for the sake of Christian faith. I refer to my God, who has sent me. I believe that the Church and Our Lord are in union—

and you should not make things so difficult for me. As for
a judgment on my works, I should not be forbidden to go
to Mass.

Seeing Joan's aggravated exhaustion, the judges pursued her for
several more hours with the same repeated questions about the
appearances of her visions and her refusal to put off male apparel. Her
answers were no different from before.

Sixteenth Session: Saturday Afternoon, March 17

During the final session of the preliminary interrogation, Joan referred
her entire case to the pope in Rome, a request that according to the law
had to be granted but was not. Instead, the bishops harassed her with
questions about her childhood, about the voices, about the propriety of
the names of Jesus and Mary on the ring she received from her parents,
and on the standard she took into battle.

Questioner: Why did you bring that standard into the church at
      Reims?
   Joan: It had endured all the trouble—it was only right that it
      shared in the honors too.

ON SUNDAY, MARCH 18, and Thursday, March 22, Cauchon summoned Beaupère, Le Maître and other assessors to his residence to
prepare the formal Articles of Indictment with which she would be
charged. On March 24 Cauchon read a summary of the interrogations to Joan in her prison cell, and she agreed it was correct but for
two minor points. The next day was Palm Sunday, and she was invit-

ed to attend Mass—if she would wear a dress. She said she would prefer to keep her male attire, and so Cauchon refused her the sacrament.

The Trial

The second phase of the trial assembled in a room adjacent to the Great Hall where proceedings had begun.

First Deliberation: Tuesday, March 27

About forty assessors gathered, but very few had attended the interrogations in Joan's cell; thus they heard what she said only as it was reflected in the charges. Joan was brought from her cell and placed in the midst of all. Cauchon began:

Questioner: The doctors gathered here are all men of the Church, educated in both human and divine law—all of us benevolent and merciful. We want to proceed with gentleness and sympathy, and we demand no punishment against you. We wish only to teach and lead you along the path of salvation. Because you are neither literate nor learned in such high matters, you may select one of us to advise you—and if you do not wish to make the choice, we would be happy to give you as many counselors as you wish, who will guide you in your answers.

Joan: First, I thank you and all here present. But as for your offer of counsel and advice, I have no intention of separating myself from the counsel of God.

Over the course of two days, March 27 and 28, the seventy Articles of Indictment were read to Joan by the chief prosecutor, Jean d'Estivet, and she was required to respond to each item. She had heard each of them before, as questions put to her during the previous weeks; now, however, they were framed with imputations of guilt deriving from falsehoods created by Cauchon and company. Joan's simple statements about her childhood, for example, and the religious education she received from her mother were twisted into fabrications that she engaged in magic, sorcery and superstition—practices falsely alleged to be widespread in Domrémy, according to the articles.

Her answers to these indictments repeated precisely what she had said earlier, and she never wavered in her convictions. Many of the seventy articles were themselves repetitious, and each had been put to her before. These are but a few examples from the formal indictment, each of them untrue according to both the facts and her claims; to each charge Joan uttered a simple, firm denial:

She has been guilty of many wicked practices. She has allowed herself to be idolized, adored, and honored. She has summoned demons and evil spirits and has made covenants with them.

Her mother was a witch and a sorceress.

She went to Neufchâteau without her parents' permission, and there she stayed in a woman's house and led an immoral life.

The young man to whom she was engaged refused to marry her because of her immoral life.

She claimed that she would bear three sons—a pope, an emperor and a king.

Her refusal to wear woman's clothing is blasphemous, heretical and a failure in submission to the will of the Church. [This article alone was rephrased and repeated no less than eighteen times.]

She promised to kill the enemies of the dauphin by magic.

She discouraged the king of France from making peace and encouraged everyone to butchery and murder.

Everything she did was achieved under the advice and with the aid of evil spirits.

She said that God loves the king of the French and hates the English.

She insists that her voices and her visions come from God, but she is unable to prove it. This reveals that they are demonic.

At this point one of the assessors interrupted, asking Joan how she prayed most recently; her response has come down to us:

> My most sweet Lord, in honor of your holy Passion, I beg You, if You love me, to reveal to me how I should answer these churchmen. As for my clothing, I know by whose command I took it, but I know not if I should put it off. Therefore, I pray that it may please You to tell me.

The indictments then continued:

She was a vicious commander in war with a lust for blood.

She wished to employ only men to serve her in the privacy of her room.

She worked only for her own material gain, for riches and honors.

She said that God had long ago deserted her.

An assessor interrupted the reading to ask:

Questioner: Will you submit to the Church Militant?

> *Joan:* I will show it all the reverence in my power. But concern-
> ing my words and deeds, I refer everything to my God, who
> has asked me to do them.

The reading of the articles concluded with a surprisingly weak summary:

> She has refused to reform her ways.

THE INQUISITORIAL PROMOTER had composed a document of counsel to the judges:

> We charge you so that a certain woman commonly called Jeanne
> be by you sentenced and declared to be a witch or sorceress, a
> diviner, a false prophetess, a conjuror of demons, a committed
> practitioner of magic. She thinks only evil of our Catholic faith,
> she is schismatic, sacrilegious, idolatrous, apostate, evil-speaking
> and evil-doing, blasphemous, scandalous, seditious, a destroyer of
> peace, a warmonger who thirsts for human blood and urges oth-
> ers to spill it. She has abandoned the decency of her sex, she
> dresses unnaturally like a man-at-arms, she betrays human and
> divine law and Church discipline, she seduces princes and people
> alike, she accepts veneration, she has contempt for God....

And so it went, a chain of absurd lies composed by churchmen for the sole purpose of advancing their own political favor by destroying an innocent. By a bitter irony, all this occurred during Holy Week.

Interrogation in the Prison: Holy Saturday, March 31

Asked if she would submit her judgment to the Church's, Joan replied:

Joan: I cannot revoke anything that has come to me from my visions and revelations, nor will I cease to do everything my Lord commands me to do. And if you tell me that my revelations are illusions or diabolical things or superstitious, I will continue to place everything in the hands of my God, whose commands I have always obeyed. Everything I have done was by God's command, and in no way could I ever have done the opposite. And if the Church Militant orders me to do the contrary, I would not submit to anyone in the world except Our Lord.

Questioner: Do you not believe that you are subject to our Holy Father the Pope, the cardinals, the archbishops, bishops, and other prelates of the Church?

Joan: I am the servant of all—but Our Lord's first.

TEN

A Matter of Honor

(April–May 1431)

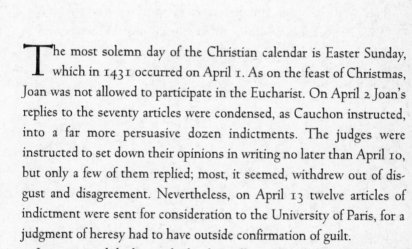

The most solemn day of the Christian calendar is Easter Sunday, which in 1431 occurred on April 1. As on the feast of Christmas, Joan was not allowed to participate in the Eucharist. On April 2 Joan's replies to the seventy articles were condensed, as Cauchon instructed, into a far more persuasive dozen indictments. The judges were instructed to set down their opinions in writing no later than April 10, but only a few of them replied; most, it seemed, withdrew out of disgust and disagreement. Nevertheless, on April 13 twelve articles of indictment were sent for consideration to the University of Paris, for a judgment of heresy had to have outside confirmation of guilt.

Joan, meanwhile, languished in her cell, growing ever more thin and pale because of the rotten diet and the pain of moving about. Her family had visited Rouen, but she was not allowed to see them. There was no word from Charles or any of his courtiers. No priest or prelate from France came to Normandy to speak on behalf of her and her achievements. She was utterly alone but for the consolation of her voices; told that they were of the devil, she too may have had momentary doubts in the small hours of the night. But if such doubts came to her, they were soon overcome.

On April 16 Joan was given a carp to eat; soon after, she began to be violently ill. Informed of her worsening condition the next morning, Bedford was fearful that she would die and thus not be subjected to the logical term of a trial by heresy. He sent to Joan his wife's physician, Jean Tiphaine, who recalled:

Jean d'Estivet led me to her, and I went in to find a few other people in her cell with her, [the physician] Guillaume de la Chambre among them. I took her pulse, asked what she felt and where she had pain. She said that the bishop of Beauvais had sent her a carp to eat and she thought this caused her illness. With that, d'Estivet became furious, called her a whore, and shouted, "You slut, you ate something to make yourself sick!" She replied that this was completely untrue, and they exchanged quite bitter words. She had been vomiting violently for quite some time.*

Guillaume de la Chambre added:

Warwick said that Joan was very ill, and on no account did the king wish her to die a natural death—she was to die only after a trial, and then by burning—and so he sent me to her with some other doctors. We examined her right side, determined that she had a fever, and decided to bleed her. This was reported to Warwick, who told us, "Be careful, for she's a cunning girl and could kill herself." Nevertheless, the bleeding was done, and she felt better. But after

---

* Would Cauchon knowingly have sent Joan a poisoned fish in order to end the proceedings with her untimely death? Such an action may not have been out of character, but there is no evidence for it; more to the point, he would have failed to secure precisely what the English wanted and what would effect his triumph—a public proclamation of her perfidy, her execution as a heretic, and the ultimate discredit of Charles VII. Given the lack of refrigeration it is likely that Joan had food poisoning with no help from the bishop of Beauvais, although we can surely understand her suspicions.

exchanging angry words with d'Estivet, who called her a whore and a tramp, Joan became very angry and fell ill again.

Weak but recovering slowly, she was stirred from a restless daze on the morning of April 18, when Cauchon and seven assessors glided into her cell. If she was unwilling to accept the Church's counsel, admonished the bishop darkly, she would be in great physical danger; this was an unsubtle threat of torture.

Joan: In light of the illness I am suffering, it seems to me that I am already in great danger of death. If that is coming, I ask you to hear my confession, give me [the Eucharist] and bury me in consecrated ground.

Questioner: If you wish the benefits of good Christian people, you must do what all good Catholics do—submit to Holy Church.

Joan: I am not able to speak with you any more today.

Questioner: If you are afraid of death on account of your illness, you ought to reform your life: you cannot die with the sacraments unless you submit.

Joan: Whatever happens to me, I will not say anything different from what I have said. I am a good Christian and I will die one.

Questioner: Wouldn't you like a fine and noble procession of people to come in and pray for you?

Joan: I will be content if good people pray to God for me.

The University of Paris scholars, however, were not kneeling on her behalf. The majority agreed with Cauchon's conclusions of guilt as expressed in the twelve articles, but some dissented and others insisted the matter be put before the pope. Simultaneously, the priests of Rouen cathedral wrote to Cauchon, informing him of their anxiety about both the legality of the trial and the fact that Joan was reported to have been deliberately confused by the reading of documents to her in Latin. There was, in other words, no unanimous decision about Joan. She was charged with insubordination by refusing to put off men's garb, and this was turned into an indictment of disobedience *to the Church*. This was certainly a feeble foundation on which to justify her condemnation and consequent execution by civil authority.

A Public Admonition: Wednesday, May 2

Dragged into the great hall because of her weakness, Joan was brought on May 2 before no less than sixty-three judges and assessors. A clever young theologian named Jean de Châtillon was instructed by Cauchon to read a lengthy summary of the twelve charges and then to ask her if she was willing to correct herself and submit to the Church.

Joan: Read what I have said before, and then I will answer you. I put my entire trust in God alone. I love Him with all my heart.

Questioner: Will you submit to the Church Militant—the authority of the Church on Earth?

Joan: I believe in the Church on Earth. As for my words and deeds, I place them all before my God, who has asked them of me.

Questioner: Have you no judge on earth? Is not the pope your judge?

Joan: I have one good Master—Our Lord, in whom, and in no other, I place all my trust.

Questioner: If you do not believe in the Church, you would be a heretic and pronounced guilty by other judges.

Joan: Even if I saw the fire being prepared, I would say only what I have already said, and nothing else.

Questioner: Will you submit to the authority of our Holy Father, the
Pope?

Joan: Take me to him, and I will reply to him.

Her words caused an uneasy mutter among the judges. Most
emphatically, Joan did not want merely a written account of her words
sent to the pope, for she knew she would be misrepresented; instead,
she wanted to appear personally in Rome for her case. "Take me to
him, and I will reply to him," by which she commended herself directly
to the pope, was an ordinary request, invariably granted to a suspected
heretic. But Cauchon could not risk papal dismissal of the charges
against her. When Manchon asked if he should note her request in the
record, the bishop replied that was not necessary. "Aha!" cried Joan,
indicating Cauchon. "You're very careful to record things against me,
but you don't want to set down anything that might do me good."[*]

Later that day Cauchon learned that Jean de la Fontaine, charged
with making the trial summaries, had gone privately to Joan along with
Isambart de la Pierre and Martin Ladvenu; they all advised her not
merely to request papal intervention but to demand it with her hand
on the Bible. This made Cauchon furious and loud with threats. La
Fontaine left Rouen and had no further dealings with the trial; Isambart and Martin were taken under the protection of Jean Le Maître.
After this Warwick and Cauchon allowed no one access to Joan except
for the usher, Jean Massieu.

There followed the usual charges concerning male clothing, which
would be the issue on which her fate was determined; questions about
her revelations; queries about her faith in the Church; and charges
about her affirmation of the Creed. By this time Joan was utterly
exhausted, wounded and beaten down by a year of imprisonment and

---

[*] Although her request for a papal audience was excised from the trial record, it was
detailed by Isambart de la Pierre during his testimony for the nullification process, on
May 9, 1452; see Duparc, *Procès en nullité*, 1:222.

ever worse treatment, by threats, malnourishment, insomnia, appalling loneliness and the belligerence of men she had been raised to respect. As a result she no longer had any stamina to spar with her judges, and she seems to have known that her cause was more futile with every hour. In the middle of this long day, her answer to each question eventually became a simple repetition—over and over, spoken wearily but in the most touchingly resolute tone:

> *Joan:* I look only to my God.

The Threat of Torture: Wednesday, May 9

Cauchon was growing ever more desperate to trap Joan into an admission of heresy; he also lost the confidence of more than a dozen clerics, who left the proceedings and never returned; they knew that threats against them uttered now would simply highlight Cauchon's apparent failure to close the case.

The bishop's next tactic took some of his colleagues by surprise. Joan was shuttled down to the castle's great dungeon, where nine judges lined a circular wall. In the midst of the damp, fetid chamber were a master executioner—in reality, a master torturer—and the common instruments by which prisoners might be subjected to unspeakable agony. After the usual admonitions and exhortations, she said:

> *Joan:* If you tore my limbs and threatened me so far as death, I would never say anything other than what I have already. And if I did so, I would later claim that you drew it out of me by force.

The man charged with torturing remembered, "I just left the room without doing anything."

Joan continued:

> *Joan:* I asked my voices if I ought to submit to the Church
> because many churchmen were urging me to do so. The
> voices promised me that the Lord would help me and that I
> should look to Him for everything. I also asked if I would
> be burned, and I was again told to wait on the Lord, and
> He would help me.

Joan was hauled back to her cell while the judges deliberated for three days the prudence of applying torture to obtain either her submission to them or an outright confession of guilt. On the afternoon of May 12 Cauchon summoned them and a few more to his home, where they took a vote: ten were against torture, three in favor of it. Accepting the wisdom that the trial would be sullied if it were known to have included torture, Cauchon abandoned the idea.

The Ruse of Jean de Luxembourg: Sunday, May 13

On the evening of Sunday, May 13, Richard de Beauchamp, Earl of Warwick, hosted a grand banquet for one hundred ten people at the castle. The guest list included Pierre Cauchon; Jean de Mailly, bishop of Noyon; Jean de Luxembourg, Joan's first captor; and the Earl of Stafford.

During the feast, Warwick—on behalf of King Henry, the Duke of Bedford and himself—informed Cauchon that Joan's trial was lasting far too long. The process was not only expensive, said Warwick, it also gave an impression of incompetence and untidiness. The English wanted Joan publicly disgraced and dramatically put to death, and soon: in this matter, Warwick complained, Cauchon had promised much but had delivered only expense sheets. The bishop's response was not noted, although he departed the festivities early that evening and, we may presume, swung into action.

After dinner Warwick led some guests to see his famous prisoner. Aimond de Macy, the Burgundian knight who had once tried to molest Joan at Beaurevoir (and got slapped for his effort), was also present; years later he described the scene and the sadistic taunting of Joan by Luxembourg:

Jean de Luxembourg wanted to see Joan, and so we went to her cell in the company of Warwick and Stafford. Once there, [Luxembourg] said to her, "Joan, I have come to ransom you, as long as you promise never to bear arms against us again." She replied, "In God's name— you're mocking me! I know very well that you have neither the will nor the ability to do this." They argued over that for a few minutes, and then she said, "I know the English want me killed, because they think that once I'm dead they will have the kingdom of France. But even if there were a hundred thousand more *goddons** than there are now, they will never have France." Stafford was so furious at Joan that he drew his dagger to strike her, but Warwick intervened.

Cauchon Announces the Paris Verdict: Saturday, May 19

By Saturday the bishop of Beauvais was in high spirits. He had his reply from the faculty at Paris, and it was, as Cauchon must have expected, precisely what he wanted. The learned university men had read the dozen articles of indictment, and although not one of them had ever met, seen or heard Joan, they were eager to have done with her. Forty-two of the

---

* To the French the English seemed constantly to utter the expletive *God damn*— hence the French nickname for them, *goddons*.

forty-seven clerics and doctors agreed, on the basis of Cauchon's report, that Joan was a heretic and ought to be handed over to the civil authorities for punishment unless she retracted everything she had ever claimed and admitted to fakery and fraudulence.

This was no surprise since the faculty at Paris had long taken the side of the English king and the Burgundians. Cauchon summoned the Rouen judges to his chapel on Saturday and had the university's conclusions read aloud. Following that, there was unanimous agreement that the opinion of Paris be proclaimed to Joan and that she be given an admonition and a final warning before judgment was pronounced.

The University Censure Is Read to Joan: Wednesday, May 23

On May 23 a young cleric named Pierre Maurice, fresh from his theological studies, read the report to Joan in a room of the castle near her cell. The response from Paris, straining to find guilt where there was none, might have been hilarious were it not so self-evidently pathetic:

Her visions were malicious fabrications and her revelations were from evil spirits;

Her belief in the voices of her angels and saints betokened an error in faith;

Her words revealed her to be superstitious, presumptuous, and proud;

Her clothing imitated the traditions of idolaters;

Her letters to which she added a cross, to indicate that instructions ought not to be followed, were blasphemous;

Her departure from home was a form of disobedience to her parents, which was scandalous;

Her leap from the tower at Beaurevoir was suicidal, and her belief that God had forgiven her was presumptuous and showed that she did not comprehend the doctrine of free will;

Her belief that she had not committed grievous sin and that she would be brought to eternal life was rash and mendacious;

Her contention that her saints favored France was blasphemy against them and a sin against the commandment to love one's neighbor, the English;

Her belief that her visions were of God, like her vow of virginity, showed that she was idolatrous and took illegal oaths;

Her refusal to submit her words and deeds to the Church, and insisting that she would be judged by God alone, demonstrated that she had no understanding of the authority of the Church.

The University of Paris concluded, with high-toned meaningless-ness, that Joan had separated herself from the true faith, that she was thus an apostate, a liar and a sorceress as well as a heretic; hence she must abjure—frankly admit—her errors and retract her claims. Failing that, she must be appropriately punished by secular authorities.

At once, at Cauchon's insistence and in the presence of some two dozen assessors, the young cleric addressed Joan in what was termed the formal charitable admonition or warning. "Joan, my very dear friend," he began, "it is now time, at the end of your trial, to think care-fully about what has been said ... for punishments shall be inflicted on you if you do not amend your words and actions and submit to the Church.... If you fail in this, your soul will be damned to eternal agony and your body will be cruelly destroyed." And so he continued, repeat-ing in detail the injunctions and the threats.

There was silence for a moment, and then Joan spoke; her verbatim reply has been preserved in the original French:

> *Joan:* Quant à mes fais et mes diz que j'ay diz eu procès, je m'y raporte et les veul soustenir: As for my actions and deeds, what I said at the trial I now repeat, and I stand by it.
>
> *Questioner:* Do you not believe that you are bound to submit your words and deeds to the Church or to anyone other than God?
>
> *Joan:* La manière que j'ai toujours dicte et tenu eu procès, je la veuil maintenir quant ad ce: What I said and maintained at my trial, I still assert now.... And if I were to be condemned, and I saw the fire set, the wood prepared, and the executioner ready to throw me into the flames, even in the midst of the fire I would say nothing other than what I have previously said. And what I have sworn I will maintain even to my death.

With that statement, Cauchon declared the trial ended, adding that sentence would be pronounced the next day; furthermore, he required everyone to gather at an appointed hour in the cemetery of Saint-Ouen.

The assessors fully expected that a punishment of life imprisonment would be pronounced for Joan's rebellion and heresy—that is, for her refusal to wear women's clothing. But Cauchon knew that the Duke of Bedford required more than life imprisonment; thus the prison sentence would be only a first step. The bishop would have to find a reason for the death penalty, and the only ground for that was relapse: a suspect, after repenting of the crimes charged, would have to fall again into precisely the same forbidden actions or habits, and this would warrant death. Cauchon had to devise an elaborate scenario.

The Abjuration: Thursday, May 24

The next day Joan was led out in chains from the castle to the walled cemetery adjoining the abbey of Saint-Ouen, where an enormous crowd had gathered, eager for excitement. Two viewing stands were prepared, one for the prelates, the other for the assessors. A stake had been fixed in the ground as a threat of execution by burning (which, Joan may not have known, could not yet be carried out).

Cauchon's friend, the impassioned theologian Guillaume Erart, then preached a long sermon addressed directly to the prisoner and condemning her harshly for her crimes. A portion of the text was also dedicated to a blunt denunciation of Charles VII, which caused Joan to leap up and shout, "Condemn me, if you will, but not the king!"

In reply, Erart laid aside his prepared text and pointed at Joan: "Your king is also a heretic and a schismatic, for he listened to you and your so-called voices."

No matter the danger of the moment, Joan remained steadfast in her loyalty to a sovereign who had done nothing to help her: "I swear to you that my king is a fine, true, and noble Christian!"

"Force her to keep silent!" shouted Erart to the guards, and then he concluded his sermon, staring directly at Joan. "Here are the judges. They have time and again invited and required you to submit your erroneous words and deeds to the judgment of the Church."

To everyone's surprise, Joan rose and in a clear voice said, "I will answer you. Regarding all my words and deeds, I appeal first of all to God." There were shouts, murmurs and much shuffling, and Joan waited for silence. "I also wish the record to be sent to Rome and put before the pope, for everything I did was at God's command."

"This is impossible, for our Holy Father is too far away. Besides, you must submit to your bishop." At that point a document was brought to Joan. "You will abjure!" shouted Erart, taking his place at Cauchon's side. "You will deny everything you have claimed, you will submit—

and you will sign this document now!" She glanced at the paper and then said what they all knew—that she could neither read nor write. "Let this paper be read by the clergy," Joan said, hoping to hear the document proclaimed aloud. "If they advise me to sign it, I shall freely do so."

"You will sign right now!" cried Erart. "Otherwise fire will consume you before this day is over!" The crowd began to shout, stones were thrown, and general chaos ensued. In the midst of the confusion Laurent Calot, the king's secretary, placed a small bench before Joan, set a paper on it, and forced a writing instrument into her hand.

Ill, exhausted after a long and bitter ordeal, and terrified at the prospect of imminent death by fire, Joan was near collapse. Massieu thought he heard her say that it was better to sign than to burn, and with Calot's hand guiding hers, she drew a circle—and put an X in it. That was taken as her signature, which may explain the recorded fact that, at that very moment, those nearby heard Joan's bitter laugh. Had she not said that such a cross indicated a document that should be ignored?

Coded or not, what exactly did Joan sign, to which crimes did she apparently admit, and to what Church demands did she give her assent?

The abjuration text that Cauchon ordered to be inserted into the official record (with the attachment of a separate paper purporting to be her signature) was a long and detailed confession of guilt. Until recently this was presumed to be the authentic abjuration of Joan of Arc:

All those who have erred and been at fault in the Christian faith and have by God's grace returned to the light of truth and unity of Our Holy Mother Church should vigilantly prevent the enemy of hell from driving them back and causing their relapse into error and damnation. Therefore I, Joan, commonly called the Maid, a miserable sinner, recognizing the snares of error in which I was held, and being by God's grace returned to Our Holy Mother Church, in

order to show that my return is made not insincerely but with a
good heart and will, I now confess that I have most grievously sinned
by falsely pretending to have had revelations and apparitions from
God, His angels, Saint Catherine, and Saint Margaret; by seducing
others; by believing foolishly and lightly; by making superstitious
divinations; by blaspheming God and His saints; by breaking the
divine law, holy Scripture, and canon law; by wearing a shameful and
immodest dress against the decency of nature, and hair cropped like
a man's, against all womanly modesty; by bearing arms; by cruelly
desiring the shedding of human blood; by declaring that I did all
these things by the command of God, His angels and saints, and
that to do so was good and not wrong; by being seditious and idolatrous, by adoring and summoning up evil spirits. I confess also that I
have been schismatic and in many ways have erred from the path.*

These crimes and errors I, by God's grace having returned to the
way of truth through the holy doctrine and good counsel of yourselves and the doctors and masters whom you sent me, sincerely and
with a good heart abjure and recant, renouncing and cutting myself
off from them all. In this I submit to the correction, disposition,
amendment, and entire decision of Our Holy Mother Church and of
your good justice. And I vow, swear and promise to you, my lord
Saint Peter, Prince of the Apostles; to our Holy Father the Pope of
Rome, his vicar and successor; to you, my lords, to the bishop of
Beauvais and the religious brother Jean Le Maître, vicar of the lord
Inquisitor of the faith, my judges, that I will never through exhorta-
tion or other means return to the aforesaid errors, from which it has
pleased God to deliver and remove me. I will always dwell in the
unity of Our Holy Mother Church and the obedience of our Holy
Father the Pope of Rome. This I say, affirm, and swear by God

---

* The mention of schism was calculated to evoke the Great Schism in the Church,
only recently resolved.

almighty and the holy gospels. In witness whereof, I sign this with my mark. —Joan.

This self-incriminating document was, however, a complete fabrication, composed later by Thomas de Courcelles under orders from Pierre Cauchon. All the eyewitnesses to that day insist that the document read to Joan was "about the length of the Lord's Prayer."

"What she signed," according to Massieu, who was at her side and whose testimony was supported by the others, "was a paper of no more than eight lines, saying that she would not again bear arms, wear men's clothing, or cut her hair. That was what I read to her. But another document, not this one, was put into the trial record. She had no idea what was on it, nor what were the consequences of signing." Such was also the testimony of no fewer than six witnesses who were present that morning, including Guillaume Manchon.

Once the paper was removed, Joan's sentence was read aloud: "life-long imprisonment … so that you may repent of your sins and never again commit them." Whatever the words Joan actually put her mark to, and however (contradictorily or not) she intended that mark, she now realized that she had given the impression that she had denied her voices, her spiritual state, her mission—in summary, her entire awareness of herself before God. At Cauchon's order she was taken back to Warwick's prison, where she put on a dress brought for her to wear and, as a sign of penance, submitted to the complete shaving of her head.

Very soon she learned that she had been deceived. The standard penalty after admitting to religious faults was a penance, perhaps a temporary imprisonment, followed by release. In any case she certainly expected, as was also the custom, to be freed from her chains and transferred to a Church facility, where she would be guarded by women. And she would surely be allowed the sacraments. But all of these expectations were futile. She was to remain chained for life as a political prisoner in an English political prison, despite the fact that a Church verdict of guilt for religious crimes had just been pronounced against her.

The English, meanwhile, were furious with Cauchon, for the sentence meant that Joan was not to be executed but incarcerated for life. Warwick wasted no time in angrily accosting Cauchon: how did he mismanage the case to the point that Joan escaped a death sentence? "My lord," said the bishop calmly to the earl, "have no fear—we shall catch her yet."

Cauchon had succeeded in making only one feeble charge stick against Joan: she had worn male clothing in defiance of his orders, and thus, he claimed, she was in rebellion against the Church itself. That this was wildly incorrect reasoning (not to say theologically imbecilic) was conveniently ignored. Her abjuration, which evidently contained a promise never again to wear male garb, would be the trap that would cause Joan's relapse—and hence bring about her execution by the secular authority. If she wore men's garb again, that would mean a reversion to the state of a heretic, from which there would be no second conversion. Execution would follow according to due process.

Sunday, May 27–Tuesday, May 29

The next several days were full of confusion, both inside and outside the prison, and the record reflects the various reminiscences of several witnesses. On crucial issues they agree, and on one point there can be no argument: when Joan was seen wearing men's clothes again, someone had to have brought them to her.

Jean Massieu gave the most elaborate account of what happened over the weekend, and his sworn testimony was based on what Joan told him the day before her death. On Sunday morning she asked her guards to remove her chains so that she might go to the latrine. "They tore off her dress as they unlocked the fetters, and they would not give it back. Instead they gave her the male clothing she had worn before. She reminded them that she was forbidden to wear that, but they removed the woman's dress—and so, compelled by necessity, she put on the male garb again. After she was seen that way all day, it became the reason why she was judged relapsed and was condemned." The entire charade, according to Massieu, was "entirely unjust."*

Cauchon's direct involvement in the events of Sunday morning— indeed, his plan for Joan's reversion to male clothing—was manifest in his otherwise inexplicable visit to Joan on Monday morning. With Le Maître and eight assessors, the bishop arrived at her cell, aware (or "informed") that she had changed her garments. Now, with witnesses present, she could be charged on the spot with relapse.

Even more important than the issue of the clothing, however, was the complete change of attitude her accusers found that Monday morning. Joan insisted that all her previous claims were true: she did hear voices, she was on a mission from God—and she had done very wrong in the cemetery by signing otherwise or giving a different impression, if indeed she did.

"I never intended to deny my apparitions, and whatever I said or did, it was because I was afraid of the fire.... My voices were from God, and everything I did was according to God's will. And I do not believe that either my God or my voices have ever deceived me."

Once again, on the matter of her faith in God's revelations to her, she was as adamant as before. She said she may have lied in order to save her life, but now she would cling to the truth even if she were to lose her life. Death was preferable to denial of who she was and what

---

* Manchon and Isambart de la Pierre testified that Joan resumed male clothing as a defense against assault by the guards, who had been treating her roughly since her return to prison. Their accounts, lacking Massieu's details, vary slightly but are not inconsistent with his. According to the official transcript Joan said that no one had forced her into men's clothes. But we have seen that Cauchon frequently ordered changes to the minutes.

she had received from God. *Responsio mortifera*, wrote Manchon in his notes at this point: "A fatal reply."

And with that, Cauchon swept regally from the cell, taking his team with him. He had won. "Farewell," he said to Warwick as he left the tower moments later. "Be of good cheer—it is done!"*

On Tuesday Cauchon summoned the judges and assessors to his chapel, where he reported that Joan the Maid had fully relapsed, that she once again claimed the voices and had resumed men's clothes. He canvassed their opinions, and most of the thirty-seven present felt that she should be given one last chance to repent. Cauchon thanked them for their effort, dismissed them and promptly ignored their recommendation. That afternoon they all received written notification that on the following day Joan would be taken to the Vieux Marché, the Old Market of Rouen, at eight in the morning. There she would be declared a relapsed and excommunicated heretic and would then be turned over to secular justice.

Execution: Wednesday Morning, May 30, 1431

Early on Wednesday morning Cauchon sent Martin Ladvenu, a Dominican friar who had been an assessor at her trial, to Joan's cell, with another Dominican, Jean Toutmouillé. She asked if Ladvenu would hear her confession and give her Holy Communion. Of this, the friars were uncertain: she was, after all, an intransigent heretic, and heretics were denied the sacraments as long as they were heretics— even unto death. The friars referred the matter to Cauchon, who said, "Give her anything she wants."

This odd reply may have had any one or more of several meanings: "She is innocent, so she should be given the sacraments"; "It does not

---

* Isambart de la Pierre and Martin Ladvenu report Cauchon's exact words: *"Farowelle, faictes bonne chière—il est faict"* (Quicherat, *Procès de condamnation*, 2:5, 8).

matter what she is given, she is a dead woman"; "I have no regard for the sacraments"; "Let us put the matter in God's hands." Whatever the bishop intended, his words certainly nullify the charge of heresy. Permitted to confess and to receive the Eucharist, she was absolved of her sin in the eyes of the Church, was no longer a relapsed heretic, and had to be at once free of the death penalty. But none of those consequences occurred. Cauchon's idea of justice continued; the trial and condemnation were merely preludes for murder.

"She received the sacrament with great devotion," according to Ladvenu. He then told her that her execution would certainly be that very day. "And when she heard the hard, cruel death that was coming, she burst into tears, crying pathetically that her body—"clean and whole and never corrupted," as she said—ought not to be consumed by flames and reduced to ashes. "If I had been in a Church prison and not guarded by my enemies, it would not have turned out this way."

Who should then arrive but Cauchon himself, for reasons that must remain as mysterious as his words earlier that morning. Did his presence indicate that he was gloating over his victory? Was he in some way apologetic? Did he wish to appease his conscience by trying to bring spiritual comfort?

"Bishop," Joan cried aloud, "I die because of you!"

"Ah, Joan," he replied calmly, "take it with patience. You will die because you did not keep faith with us and because you have returned to your sorcery."

"If you had put me in the prison of a Church court and handed me over to competent churchmen, this would never have happened, and you know it."

Cauchon departed, and Joan turned to one of the friars. "Where shall I be tonight?"

"Have you no faith in Our Lord?"

"With God's help, I shall be with Him in paradise."

At eight o'clock Joan was taken, wearing a long white garment and a white bonnet, to the Place du Vieux-Marché, near the church of Saint-Sauveur, where a vast crowd had gathered. Cauchon took his place with Jean Le Maître and others of the trial, and then a long sermon was preached by Nicholas Midi about her wicked ways and the opportunities she had been given to repent. "We admonished Joan ... but she remained obstinate, and had maliciously and falsely shown that she was contrite. She blasphemed God and showed herself an incorrigible heretic who had relapsed into error and is unworthy of any pity."

The English were impatient for the finale. "Priest," shouted one, "will we be home in time for dinner?"

"Joan, go in peace," concluded Midi. "The Church can no longer defend you and so dismisses you into secular hands."

Cauchon hurried on to the official sentence:

We, Pierre, by divine pity the humble bishop of Beauvais, and we, Jean Le Maître, deputy Inquisitor of the Faith, do hereby declare: Since you, Joan, called the Maid, have been found by us to have relapsed into errors and crimes of schism, idolatry, invocation of devils, and various other wickednesses ... you have incurred the sentence of excommunication. Seated on our tribunal of justice, we do cast you forth and reject you from the communion of the Church as an infected limb, and hand you over to secular justice, praying them to treat you with kindness and humanity with respect to your life and limbs.

The final statement, a procedural formality, was the last thing Cauchon wanted, and so he orchestrated a swift end to the morning's event. It was customary for such a prisoner to be officially turned over to the secular court, who would deliberate on a sentence and then decide the time, appropriateness and place of punishment. But as he had done for months, Cauchon ignored the proprieties for an Inquisitorial trial. He simply nodded to the bailiff, and the eager English, coached in advance by Bedford, Warwick and others, raced to their task.

To save time and obviate last-minute objections, everything had been neatly prepared—the stake was firmly placed in the ground in the center of the marketplace; the logs and kindling were in place; torches were ready to light the pyre; the guards had swords and lances drawn in case of public outcry; and the chains had been brought from Joan's cell, the better to fix her to the stake and prevent her, whom some believed to be a witch, from taking flight into the air.

The end happened with heartbreaking cruelty.

As she was led away and saw the apparatus of her execution, Joan collapsed, trembling and weeping. She tried to compose herself, knelt on the ground, and asked everyone to pray for her; faithful to the spirit of her Lord, she then forgave those responsible for what was happening. A paper hat was rudely placed on her head with the legend, "Heretic—Relapsed—Apostate—Idolatress." The roar of the crowd, abetted by Burgundian loyalists, grew deafening around her.

Was she aware that her mother and father were somewhere in the throng, surrounded by neighbors who had come with them from Domrémy? Isabelle and Jacques, broken and bitter, had been forbidden to see their daughter in prison; indeed, they had not seen her for more than two years. At their last meeting Joan had been a buoyant, optimistic, healthy seventeen-year-old, serious in matters of piety but often merry and always full of common sense, unassailable loyalty, and good cheer. If they were close enough to their daughter now, they saw a nineteen-year-old aged by time and chance, drawn and ill, defeated and rejected by all those to whom she had devoted her energy and her ideals.

Death by burning was considered so dreadful that there was a so-called merciful gesture performed just as the fire was lit: the executioner climbed a ladder behind the stake and either cut the throat or strangled the victim to death. This was not done to Joan, who endured a protracted torture and death because the pyre was built unusually high, for all to see.

An English guard, touched by her plight, took two sticks from the bundle at his feet, tied them together in the form of a cross, and handed it to Joan, who put it underneath her garment, close to her breast. She was then dragged up and chained to the stake, praying aloud constantly. "She never ceased to commend herself to God," said Guillaume Manchon. Isambart de la Pierre ran to a nearby church and brought back a processional cross, which he held high before her eyes.

The fire and smoke, lambent and smoldering, took their deadly time. According to the record, very many people in the crowd no longer cheered and whistled but instead began to protest, weeping and fainting at the sight and sound of such horrifying agony.

With her last breath, Joan of Arc sang out the name of her Lord Jesus. Her head slowly bowed, and her shackled body slumped against the stake.

The market square was suddenly subdued. For a long while that morning, there was the hiss and crackle of flame and wood, and then there was silence.

Afterword

"I was anxious and disturbed for a month after her death," said Guillaume Manchon. "With some of the money I received for my work as notary, I bought a prayer book, and I kept her memory alive every day in my prayers for her."

Within hours of Joan's death, one of her judges, Jean Alespée, a priest in Rouen, confided to a friend that he lamented his participation in her trial: "I wish that my soul could now be where that woman's soul is." Jean Tressart, secretary to the king of England in Rouen, tried to drown his sorrow by racing to a nearby tavern, where he spent many hours and a good deal of money: "We are lost, for we have burned a good and holy person," he wept, stopping anyone who would listen. When his remark circulated around town, he had to flee for his safety's sake; very soon those who held less prestigious positions than Tressart knew that it was in their best interest to keep quiet if they shared his feelings.

The Earl of Warwick was not among the mourners. To prevent the collection of relics, he ordered Joan's ashes to be tossed into the Seine. A week later the king of England wrote to all the princes of Christendom, a letter drafted or edited by the Duke of Bedford on behalf of nine-year-old Henry VI. The document celebrated "the just punishment suffered for her faults by a certain lying prophetess who appeared in our kingdom of France."

The usual specious charges against Joan were repeated, with the astonishing claim that England wished no vengeance against her but rather had insisted on a Church trial "for the honor of God." The letter was remarkable for outright lies: "She spurned the judgment of Our Holy Father the Pope." A similar epistle was sent four weeks later to the bishops and nobles of all occupied France, and by royal decree sermons and processions were held everywhere in joyful praise of Joan's execution. Such observances were also aimed to suppress the actions of any potential supporters or imitators.

Her death took a catastrophic toll on her father's health: within months Jacques d'Arc fell ill and died of grief, according to a firmly maintained tradition. Joan's mother, Isabelle, returned to Domrémy; she had lost her husband, both daughters and her oldest son, Jacques. Isabelle later settled in Orléans, where she was lovingly attended by neighbors and received a stipend from the crown for the rest of her life. According to some sources, Joan's brother Pierre accompanied Isabelle; Jean, it seems, sought his own fortune elsewhere, later exploiting his sister's fame in order to obtain dubious political favors.

"Her brief appearance on the political scene had extraordinary repercussions," wrote the French historian Georges Duby, who had little regard for Joan as a mystic or a saint. "Although she had died, with her intervention the tide had suddenly and miraculously turned. Despair was banished, and even her death could not check the movement she had initiated. It was to lead to the liberation of France from English occupation."

The Hundred Years' War rumbled along for another twenty-two years, but despite all the English bluster during the summer of Joan's death, fortune favored the French. The coronation of the ten-year-old Henry VI as king of France, held at Notre-Dame Cathedral on December 16, 1431, did not gain him the allegiance of more French people or solidify his position in France. Indeed, English soldiers began to desert their armies, resistance forces against the occupiers arose throughout France, and peasants who had been armed by the English turned against them. On one side, Joan's insistence on frontal assaults was retained, and it improved France's ongoing military tactics; on the other, the reign of Henry VI was severely weakened by military blunders and, inevitably, by the death of the Duke of Bedford in September 1435.

Three months later, the Treaty of Arras established a lasting peace between Charles VII and Philip of Burgundy. In 1437 Charles triumphantly took Paris and in 1449 Rouen. This effectively ended the English occupation, and by the end of 1453 no French city was in their hands. Joan's goal was finally realized: always regretting that foreign troops had been brought over to die in France, she would have heartily rejoiced when the last English soldiers returned home.

As for her king, Charles VII succeeded in mastering both English and papal influence and became a leader who left his country in far better condition than when he was crowned. A complex man, difficult to comprehend and not always sympathetic, he genuinely preferred peace to war; he freely pardoned towns that had collaborated with the English; and he was a major architect of the movement toward a united France. When he died in 1461 at the age of fifty-eight, Charles VII was widely mourned—not least because of his successful efforts to reverse the judgment against Joan the Maid.

Pierre Cauchon, who had his eye on ever more powerful positions in Church and state, was bitterly disappointed when he was denied the bishopric of Rouen and given instead the relatively insignificant see of Lisieux. Still, he was not without influence at the English court as long as it resided in France. Cauchon accumulated incalculable wealth as a partisan of Henry VI in the years to come, but he became a bitter, anxious man. In 1442, when he was about seventy-two, the man who without irony styled himself "the humble bishop of Beauvais" was being shaved by his barber when he felt something like a tight fist in his chest; a moment later, wide-eyed and breathless, he slid from the chair.

Other major clerics from the trial suffered more than a swift demise. Jean d'Estivet, one of Joan's cruelest and most implacable judges, was murdered under strange and doubtful circumstances in 1438; his body was discovered in a Rouen sewer. Nicholas Midi, author of the twelve articles of condemnation and preacher of the last sermon against Joan, died of leprosy the same year as Cauchon.

Joan's great friend, Jean d'Alençon, led an unhappy life after the king sabotaged their friendship. For years the duke continued in battle for the Valois, but he made an unfortunate decision in arranging his daughter's marriage to an English nobleman. Charles VII was extremely displeased, and then Alençon seems to have undergone a complete and inexplicable change of personality. He supported a revolt against Charles; he began to drink heavily; and he led an altogether louche life, dabbling in black magic and consorting with notorious companions. All this was so out of character for this once good and decent man that mental illness should not be discounted as an explanation.

Alençon testified generously and warmly on Joan's behalf at her nullification trial in 1456, but immediately thereafter the king had him arrested for treason. He was twice condemned to death and twice had his sentence overturned, but he spent many years in prison. Joan's *beau duc*, Jean d'Alençon, died not in chains but nevertheless bitter, lonely and unwell in 1476, at the age of sixty-nine. He had not seen his friend Joan since he was twenty-two.

When Charles VII recaptured Rouen in 1449, he learned the details of Joan's execution and probably read a copy of the trial record, which was kept at the bishop's residence. In February 1450 he set up a formal inquiry into the legality of the proceedings against her. Investigations and numerous interviews in Rouen soon made it clear that the trial had been markedly discriminatory, biased and partisan (not to say illegal). Charles was not motivated so much by gratitude to Joan or a desire for justice as he was driven by the need to validate his own status: vindicating Joan and proclaiming her innocent of any heresy, the king would effectively ratify his legitimate position on the throne of France. But her condemnation had come from a Church trial, and only the Church could retract, overturn or nullify the original verdict. Still, the groundwork could be laid.

Seven witnesses were heard on March 4 and 5, among them the notary Guillaume Manchon; Isambart de la Pierre and Martin Ladvenu, who were with Joan at her execution; and the trial usher, Jean Massieu. But there the matter stopped. Two years later Cardinal Guillaume d'Estouteville, French representative for Pope Nicholas V, heard a petition sent by Isabelle d'Arc. Another formal inquiry was undertaken, but like that of 1450 it was short-lived—and for the same reason: fear of opposing both the English (still in France) and the Church authorities.

In 1452 the new Inquisitor of France, Jean Bréhal, agreed to join d'Estouteville at a further inquiry in Rouen.

More witnesses gave evidence from May 2 to 22 that year, and the result was astonishing to the new commission. The corruption of the trial became clear, as did the lack of freedom of the judges and notaries to act. Joan's lack of counsel went against the custom of Inquisitorial trials. The details of her imprisonment were horrifying, as was the basic cause of the entire trial—the English desire to get rid of Joan and thus to discount the legitimacy of Charles's kingship.

In 1455 Pope Nicholas V died. His successor, Calixtus III, ordered the matter to be pursued that June, after Joan's mother and brothers appealed to him for justice. On November 7 the elderly, frail Isabelle Romée, accompanied by friends, traveled to Paris from her home in Orléans. In evident physical pain and emotional distress but with an impressively strong voice, she appeared before a tribunal of clergy and bishops in the grandeur of Notre-Dame Cathedral and asked that her daughter's good name be cleared of the heinous charges that condemned her to death.

Isabelle's formal statement has been preserved; in the mother's strength we hear something of the daughter:

I had a daughter born in lawful wedlock, who grew up amid the fields and pastures. I had her baptized and confirmed and brought her up in the fear of God. I taught her respect for the traditions of the Church, and I succeeded so well that she spent much of her time in church, and after going to confession, she received the Eucharist frequently. Because the people suffered so much, she had a great compassion for them in her heart, and despite her youth she would fast and pray for them with great devotion and fervor. She never thought, spoke or did anything against the faith.

But certain enemies had her arraigned in a religious trial. Despite her disclaimers and appeals, both tacit and expressed, and without any help given to her defense, she was put through a perfidious, violent, iniquitous and sinful trial. The judges condemned her falsely, damnably and criminally and put her to death in a cruel manner by fire. I demand that her name be restored.

Ten days later, on November 17, 1455, a new commission met, headed by Inquisitor Jean Bréhal and the bishops of Reims and Paris as Judges of the Appeal. They were careful to set forth the independent nature of the court and would brook no interference from king or prelate, foreign or domestic. On December 12 the trial opened, but only the d'Arc family was represented by counsel; no one came forward to speak for the accused assessors or on behalf of the late Jean d'Estivet. The case was further helped when the nephews of Pierre Cauchon announced publicly that they wanted nothing to do with the present or previous trial, for they were either not born or were very young when it occurred. But apparently they knew more than they said, for the Cauchon family asked the court that, whatever the outcome of the new inquiry, they be treated under the terms of the amnesty granted by Charles after the reconquest of Normandy.

Thus began an intensive and extensive inquiry, during which thousands of pages of documents were assembled and sworn testimony was taken from over one hundred twenty-five witnesses in Domrémy, Vaucouleurs, Orléans, Paris and Rouen—among them nobles, farmers, soldiers, neighbors of Joan and her family, ordinary citizens from each region, bishops and priests. They were all protected by the amnesty Charles VII had guaranteed to former or perceived enemies who had once taken sides against him.

At the outset Guillaume Manchon contributed not only his recollections but also his original French notes of the trial. He testified under oath that at Cauchon's order, Joan's comments were recast unfavorably (as she herself once said); furthermore, Manchon insisted that the trial was from the first a fraud and that the judges would not have treated Joan the same way if she had been English. Jean Tiphaine, one of the doctors who attended the imprisoned Joan when she fell ill in April 1431, quoted "an important Englishman" who said of Joan, "She is truly a fine woman. If only she were English!" Dunois and Alençon too were heard speaking at length of their friend and comrade-in-arms. Almost everything we know of Joan's origins, her childhood and her journey to Vaucouleurs is contained in those interviews, which (among others from the nullification trial) have been liberally cited in this book.

In addition, the judges admitted into evidence the alterations, additions and omissions in the minutes of the original trial as well as the comments made by University of Paris scholars who took exception to the twelve articles as presented to them. The incompetence of the Rouen judges, their weaknesses and prejudices and the threats of Cauchon against them, also came to light, as did the details of the dreadful treatment Joan received during the last year of her life—culminating with the illegal sentence and unlawful execution.

The trial of nullification, as it is properly called, proceeded during the winter and spring of 1456. Finally, on July 7 of that year, the trial of 1431—the trial of condemnation—was itself condemned by the pope's own appellate court in, of all places, the bishop's residence at Rouen. This was a solemn and memorable event, as the presiding bishops dramatically symbolized the corruption and malfeasance of the 1431 trial by tearing to shreds a copy of the original trial document. Isabelle attended a similar ritual at Orléans; she died two years later, on November 28, 1458.

It is important to note, however, that the nullification trial condemned no one by name, nor was there any identification of the prelates who were themselves guilty; reference is made only to "certain men." In addition, nothing was done to glorify Joan, although for many people that was implicit in her exoneration. The concluding statements of the new trial emphasized the illegality and injustice of the original, but care was taken not to exalt or venerate a young woman whose attitude to the institutional Church was far less docile than what prelates demanded and expected.

For the rest of the fifteenth century Joan was for the most part a local heroine, honored mostly in Orléans by festivals in celebration of their liberation in 1429. By the time of the eighteenth-century Enlightenment, she was a figure of embarrassment to cool-headed French atheists and agnostics. Voltaire ridiculed Joan's virginity, and his era generally regarded her as a curiosity from a dim, superstitious past. The accounts of the Hundred Years' War had not yet been widely circulated, and the trial documents and other contemporaneous accounts were left to collect dust until serious research was undertaken in the nineteenth century.

Later, left-wing politicians and an impressive list of socialists transformed Joan into a daughter of the people, a social activist with no interest in the spiritual life. Equally out of balance are those on the extreme right, sustained by prejudice and xenophobia, who claim that her piety validates a kind of French preeminence.

Joan objected to the possibility of a vanished France, absorbed into the English empire. She took no stand against including a variety of peoples speaking many languages and representing a colorful palette of historical antecedents, from Anglophilic Normandy to Celtic Brittany, from the Spanish Pyrenees to Italianate Provence, from the Germanic eastern borders to the Flemish northern regions—all of them part of what eventually became a unified France. Indeed, she knew people from all these regions.

As we have seen, it was precisely this developing sense of nationhood, quite against empire building, to which Joan responded and which her actions reinforced. As the historian Siobhan Nash-Marshall has succinctly stated, "There was no real kingdom of France" when

Joan came on the scene. Instead France was "a series of counties, duch-ies, and baronies, and the people of France were loyal to their counts, dukes and barons.... The lack of a real sense of nationhood also explains why the people of France did not constantly rebel at the pros-pect of falling under English rule."

Somehow her arrival on the scene altered the situation, and her achievements were a critical element in the foundation of French national consciousness—and indeed of the belief in the sovereignty of all nations. Joan claimed the loyalty of thousands whose depression she lifted by a unified desire to throw off the yoke of England. "Joan," Nash-Marshall added, "taught her people to rise above their petty con-cerns and provincialism and see that there was a larger unity that needed to be made out of each of the provinces of France ... [and] she proclaimed that the larger unity was a sacred thing—that it was a response to a divine calling."

If Joan was right in her insistence that the unwarranted takeover of one country by another is repugnant, then she is more than a historical curiosity: she remains a prophetic witness for every generation.

In the twentieth century especially, Joan was subjected to a variety of obsessions and passed through the prisms of those with modern preoc-cupations; thus she was written about and spoken of as if she had been a working-class radical, a warmonger, a closeted lesbian, a biological androgyne, or a pathologically frigid maiden, regardless of the lack of evidence for any such assertions. The English writer Vita Sackville-West, for example, claimed that Joan was obviously homosexual, for the record tells that when accepting hospitality from families, she pre-ferred to sleep with women rather than with men. But in the fifteenth century young and single women routinely shared a bed with one another for mutual protection against attack.

Those with a different agenda point to her military career as a sign of Joan's sexual confusion, which is perhaps too antique and pathetic an objection to justify rebuttal. At the extreme of the theories concerning

Joan's presumed mental aberration is the assertion that she had tuberculosis of the brain from drinking raw cow's milk. The only possible conclusion to this position is that if tuberculosis of the brain can produce such marvelous results for a country and a people, we ought immediately to ban the pasteurization of milk. As for her remarkable physical and emotional courage, it was always complemented by admirable common sense and an unhysterical piety that was rooted in a belief that God cares about His world.

In historiography, dramatic literature, fiction, art, music and film, Joan has been an endlessly appealing subject. Four years after her death the first of several plays was staged at Orléans, with a huge cast of characters that included Joan, the Virgin Mary, Saint Michael and God Himself. French chronicles noted the importance of her actions in booting out the English, which eventually led to the end of the Hundred Years' War; the chronicles did not, however, believe that she was sent by God. The poet François Villon, who was born the year Joan died, mentioned her favorably in his *Ballade des femmes du temps jadis* as "*la bonne Lorraine / Qu'Anglois bruslèrent à Rouen*," the good girl from Lorraine whom the English burned at Rouen. But by the eighteenth century Voltaire knew his readers would accept his satiric portrait of Joan as a village idiot.

Things changed later, however: in the nineteenth century no fewer than eighty-two French plays sympathetic to Joan were performed, some of them wildly altering the facts of her life, and at least two operas (by Gounod and by Mermet) were enormously successful. In the twentieth century poets, historians and playwrights inevitably turned to her for inspiration, and in 1909 alone (the year she was beatified) seventeen plays were written and produced. After her canonization as Saint Joan of Arc in 1920, there followed no fewer than thirty-nine dramatic works (counting only up to 1986). Some were pious pageants for schoolchildren; others were serious reflections on patriotism, ethics, national identity or the primacy of conscience. Notable examples were Charles Péguy's triptych, *Le Mystère de la charité de Jeanne d'Arc;* Paul Claudel's verses for *Jeanne d'Arc au bûcher* were set to music by Arthur Honegger, and the work remains an oratorio in the standard canon, and Jean Anouilh's play *L'Alouette* was a great success in France and later in America as *The Lark.*

Librarians list more than four hundred plays, cantatas, symphonies, tone poems and hymns about Joan of Arc, and archivists can name more than three hundred paintings, statues and engravings—a catalog that makes her by far the most celebrated person in artistic history. French painters have also been drawn to Joan's story: Ingres, Bastien-Lepage, Carrière and Millais, for example, all created memorable works that have withstood the tests of time and fashion.

As might be expected, the early English histories simply dismissed Joan as a common witch. Shakespeare summarized that view in *Henry VI, Part One,* wherein Joan is little more than a violent, sluttish fiend who depends on the powers of darkness, which finally fail her. Such was the conventional wisdom about Joan until, at the end of the eighteenth century, Robert Southey wrote a long epic poem praising her.

Perhaps the most enthusiastic and best known English celebration is George Bernard Shaw's play *Saint Joan.* Shaw's heroine is a sturdy girl, only marginally religious, socially left-wing, intellectually clever and the first Protestant.

How far the English view of Joan has come since Shakespeare may be read in the words of no less a patriot than Winston Churchill, who memorably wrote,

Joan was a being so uplifted from the ordinary run of mankind that she finds no equal in a thousand years. She embodied the natural goodness and valour of the human race in unexampled perfection. Unconquerable courage, infinite compassion, the virtue of the simple, the wisdom of the just, shone forth in her. She glorifies as she freed the soil from which she sprang.

In Germany, Schiller's *Maid of Orleans* featured a mixed-up bumpkin in a monumental kind of Teutonic soap opera: men fall madly in love with her, and she almost succumbs until, after being captured, she breaks her chains and dies fighting alongside her king—not at the stake, not at the hands of clerics.

Joan was also the subject of an Italian opera by none other than Giuseppe Verdi. The libretto laments the waste of her virginity and is concerned mostly with Joan's reconciliation with her suspicious father. At the end, as in Schiller, Joan escapes her confinement and dies, beautifully and cleanly, in battle. Tchaikovsky's Russian opera is similarly dismissive of historical facts.

Mark Twain's *Personal Recollections of Joan of Arc* was a highly successful American novel about Joan and a wildly uncharacteristic work. Twain spent years researching the latest documentary evidence available at the end of the nineteenth century, and the result was a deeply moving novel. Agnostic misanthrope though he was, Twain considered this book very much his best work, and so it may be. He obviously loved Joan and insisted that she was the most magnificent, virtuous, thoroughly admirable person in the history of the world. His awe is evident in the writing.

American playwright Maxwell Anderson's *Joan of Lorraine* presented an interesting conceit immediately after World War II: the play is about a troop of actors rehearsing a play about Joan, and therefore there is plenty of opportunity for reflections on the nature of compromise—in art and in trials, just as in battle, ethics and all of life.

One of the first films ever made, in 1898, was about Joan of Arc, and producers, directors and actors have since then found her story irresistible. At least fifty-three feature films have reached the screen, directed by, among others, Cecil B. DeMille, Carl Dreyer, Victor Fleming,

Roberto Rossellini, Otto Preminger, Robert Bresson and Jacques Rivette. Documentary films about her are legion.

Joan of Arc is certainly an example of the victimized political prisoner, of the hostage unjustly taken, betrayed by those to whom she was devoted, oppressed by those who place power before people. Lonely in her suffering, terrified in the face of a dreadful death, she was at last a sacrifice to a suffocating kind of fanaticism.

Religious, psychological, philosophical and literary theories about Joan of Arc are still stockpiled, given new twists, sifted, discarded and taken up again. But perhaps the essential "truth" about her is captured in an affecting and powerful image—that of a country girl in her family's garden, listening silently in the presence of the living God. Improbably, she becomes the sign that God is free to act as He wills to act, not as we presume He ought to act. Contrary to all expectations, she is a reminder that God in His mercy often chooses the least obvious people for greatness. His freedom is reflected in hers, for she responds in complete trust. Perhaps Joan makes no sense without this leap of faith in the divine ingenuity.

Joan of Arc, with her radical and incandescent confidence in God and her unshakable belief in His love for the integrity of every nation, continues to claim our attention in the work of historians, philosophers, theologians and biographers; in the tropes of poets, playwrights and novelists; in the creative imagination of painters, composers and filmmakers. Almost six hundred years after her death at the age of nineteen, there is no indication that she will quietly disappear.

Acknowledgments

This book could not have been written without the cooperation and assistance provided by personnel at the following archives and libraries: in Paris, the Centre Historique des Archives Nationales, the Bibliothèque Nationale and the Bibliothèque de l'Assemblée Nationale; in Orléans, the Bibliothèque Municipale and the Centre Jeanne d'Arc; in London, the British Library; in Copenhagen, the Royal Library, the National Library of Denmark and the University Library of Copenhagen.

I am equally grateful for the assistance of the International Joan of Arc Society/Société Internationale de l'étude de Jeanne d'Arc, a treasury of scholarly information gathered by professors, independent scholars and students.

Among the scholars who have enriched our knowledge and perceptions of Joan, I am grateful to several who took time to answer crucial questions: Kelly DeVries, Loyola College (Baltimore, Maryland); Siobhan Nash-Marshall, College of St. Thomas (St. Paul, Minnesota); and Jane Marie Pinzino, University of Pennsylvania (Philadelphia).

My niece, Ann-Britt Elvin Andersen, enabled me to have quick access to rare volumes at the Royal Library, Copenhagen.

Irene Mahoney, OSU, replied generously and extensively to my questions about religious life in the Middle Ages.

The producer and director Pamela Mason Wagner kindly provided a copy of her magnificent documentary, *Joan of Arc—Child of War, Soldier of God* (2005).

I am very fortunate indeed to be represented by my dear friend and agent of thirty years, Elaine Markson. I would have no career at all, or at least a far less happy one, without Elaine and her colleagues—Gary Johnson, Geri Thoma and Julia Kenny. It was they who introduced me to Gideon Weil at HarperSanFrancisco—as enthusiastic and support-ive an editor as any writer could hope to find. His intelligent and specific observations much improved the text, and his friendship cheered my work at every stage. Carolyn Allison-Holland was an expert production editor, and Priscilla Stuckey my keen-eyed and graceful copyeditor.

In all my tasks and projects, I am sustained daily by the love and unfailing support of Ole Flemming Larsen, with whom I share my life.

THE NAME ON the dedication page is that of a film and television pro-ducer with a long list of credits. Respected by collaborators, admired by directors, and esteemed by everyone who has the good fortune to work with her, Sue Jett is a woman of keen insights and deep sympathies. Courageous and generous, she would very quickly have secured the affection of Joan of Arc. My life is much the better for Sue's loyalty and confidence, her leavening humor and enduring friendship—and for the happy times I share with her and her husband, Paul Elliott, a remark-ably artistic cinematographer with equally impressive credits. I am more grateful than I can say.

Notes

⛨

NOTES TO CHAPTER ONE: OF WAR AND OCCUPATION

On Jacques d'Arc and the family, see esp. Pernoud and Clin, *Joan of Arc*, 221–22. On the name Darc or d'Arc, see esp. Doncoeur, in *Nouvelles Littéraires*, no. 1198 (1950). On the children of Jacques and Isabelle, see de Bouteiller and de Braux, *Nouvelles récherches*, 3–46, and Morel, "La noblesse de la famille."

In my country: Trial session, Feb. 21, 1431.

On Joan's age: According to a sworn statement made by her childhood friend Hauviette on January 28, 1456, Joan was "three or four years older than I" (Duparc, *Procès en nullité*, 1:275), and Hauviette was born in 1411. If, then, Joan was born in 1407 or 1408, she would have been not nineteen but twenty-three or twenty-four at the time of her death. Perhaps we should be as unfussy about the matter as were Joan and her contemporaries. In any case, the weight of evidence for Joan's birth in 1412 is persuasive; see, for example, Pernoud and Clin, 27–29.

historiographers and chroniclers: Pernoud, 27.

faithful Catholics: Duparc, *Procès en nullité*, 1:253.

Sometimes she went off: Duparc, *Procès en nullité*, 1:253.

good and sweet: Duparc, *Procès en nullité*, 1:275, 185.

When I was sick: Duparc, *Procès en nullité*, 1:280.

willingly gave alms: Duparc, *Procès en nullité*, 1:282.

NOTES TO CHAPTER TWO: VISIONS

On the Great Western Schism, see, for example, McBrien, *Lives of the Popes*, 248ff.

Bloated with pride: Fatula, *Catherine of Siena's Way*, 189.

a voice from God ... a great deal of light: Joan spoke of her voices and visions extensively, for the first time, under interrogation (on Feb. 22, 1431, the second day of her trial).

I do not recognize: Feb. 27, 1431.

she said she would do better: Mar. 3, 1431.

I hear voices: Shaw, *Saint Joan*, 59.

The image of Christ spoke to him: Armstrong, Hellmann, and Short, *Francis of Assisi*, 2:76, 249.

I saw the Lord: Isaiah 6:1–8.

Every idea of Him: Lewis, *Letters to Malcolm*, 84.

NOTES TO CHAPTER THREE: TOMORROW, NOT LATER

working around: Duparc, *Procès en nullité*, 1:296.

She said she had come: Duparc, *Procès en nullité*, 1:305.

the only time she disobeyed: March 12, 1431.

On the history of Joan in art see, for example, Pernoud and Clin, *Joan of Arc*, 242–43.

as long as it should be pleasing: Joan, at the eighth session of her trial (May 12, 1431).

She then said: See Pernoud's rendering, Pernoud and Clin, 38.

For the dialogue between Joan and Jean de Metz, see Duparc, *Procès en nullité*, 1:289–90.

For Catherine Le Royer's recollections, see Duparc, *Procès en nullité*, 1:298.

Tomorrow rather than later: *Plutôt aujourd'hui que demain; et demain que plus tard*: Testimony of Jean de Metz: Duparc, *Procès en nullité*, 1:290.

There is an ongoing debate about the precise date of Joan's departure from Vaucouleurs and her arrival at Chinon; the dates given here may be the most likely.

Joan's letters to her parents and to Charles VII have not survived, but they are mentioned, respectively, at the trial sessions of Mar. 12 and Feb. 27, 1431.

NOTES TO CHAPTER FOUR: ARMOR AND A HOUSEHOLD

Jean Fouquet's portrait of Charles VII hangs in the Louvre.

turned upside down: From Chastellain's *Chroniques*, cited in Pernoud and Clin, *Joan of Arc*, 167.

My most eminent Lord: Duparc, *Procès en nullité*, 1:326.

radiant: Duparc, *Procès en nullité*, 1:400.

I was continuously: Duparc, *Procès en nullité*, 1:364.

She asked me: Duparc, *Procès en nullité*, 1:386–87.

She spoke in: Duparc, *Procès en nullité*, 1:471–72.

On the lost documents from the Poitiers interrogation, see Wood, "Joan of Arc's Mission."

The king should not reject: Quicherat, *Procès de condamnation*, 3:391–92.

became part of her mission: Wood, "Joan of Arc's Mission," 21; see also Pernoud and Clin, *Joan of Arc*, 235–36.

Of Joan's letter to the English commanders at Orléans, there are several versions with minor variations: the edition inserted into the condemnation transcript is in ms. 1119 at the Bibliothèque de l'Assemblée Nationale, Paris; another is found in the *Journal du Siège d'Orléans;* and a third is in Thomassin's *Régistre Delphinal.* The latter two may be read in Quicherat, *Procès de condamnation.*

She should have: Willard, *Christine de Pizan*, 150.

I am indebted to Jean-Claude Colrat, *Compagnons d'armes*, for much of the historical background of ranks, arms, companions, etc.

Joan's parents: Duparc, *Procès en nullité*, 1:388ff.

Twice a day: Duparc, *Procès en nullité*, 1:474ff.

[Joan's] imposition: Nicolle, *Orléans 1429*, 24.

I heard many: Duparc, *Procès en nullité*, 1:370.

NOTES TO CHAPTER FIVE: THE NEW DEBORAH

On Orléans, its siege and history, see esp. Pernoud and Clin, *Joan of Arc*, 226–27.

To describe this series: Nicolle, *Orléans 1429*, 30. The siege of Orléans and its relief have been voluminously chronicled in contemporary writings and a vast literature in the last five centuries. A good and accurate treatment, with helpful maps, has been published by Nicolle, to whose work—as to that of Frances Gies—I am much indebted in this chapter.

Are you the bastard: Duparc, *Procès en nullité*, 1:318.

On the matter of Joan's religious mission, see esp. Hughson, "Joan, L'Agent Provocateur," 59–62. On Joan's appeal to others' loyalty, see DeVries, "A Woman as Leader of Men." On the religious devotion of Joan's time, DeVries offers a helpful bibliography at the end of his essay.

she brought action: DeVries, "A Woman as Leader of Men," 8.

Like it or not: Duparc, *Procès en nullité*, 1:327, 319.

They regained their courage: Duparc, *Procès en nullité*, 1:321 and 4:6.

and all the people: Duparc, *Procès en nullité*, 1:332 and 4:17–18.

NOTES TO CHAPTER SIX: "I WON'T FLY AWAY!"

to the king … (and the footnote): Duparc, *Procès en nullité*, 1:321.

Joan, won't you please: Duparc, *Procès en nullité*, 1:323.

Daughter of God: Duparc, *Procès en nullité*, 1:323. The original fifteenth-century French, recalled by Dunois, has retained a much-loved place in Joan's history: "*Fille Dé, va, va, va, je serai à ton aide, va.*"

Don't worry: Duparc, *Procès en nullité*, 1:384.

certain that God: Duparc, *Procès en nullité*, 1:383.

It had seemed premature: Duparc, *Procès en nullité*, 1:384.

She said she was afraid: Duparc, *Procès en nullité*, 1:279.

When he came toward me: Trial session of Mar. 3, 1431.

Some of the details of the coronation were given in a letter to Charles's wife, Marie d'Anjou, and her mother, Yolande d'Aragon: dated at Reims, July 17, 1429. See Colrat, *Compagnons d'armes*, vol. 1.

evokes the grandeur: Pernoud and Clin, *Joan of Arc*, 68.

On Christine de Pisan's "Le Ditié de Jehanne d'Arc," see Kennedy and Varty, eds., *Ditié de Jehanne d'Arc*.

On the views of Joan's claims and the integrity of nations, see Nash-Marshall, "On the Fate of Nations," and the same author's *Joan of Arc: A Spiritual Biography*, 143–64.

a light to the gentiles: see, for example, Isaiah 42:6 and 49:6; Acts of the Apostles 13:47 and 26:23.

NOTES TO CHAPTER SEVEN: A LEAP OF FAITH

I wish it were God's will: Duparc, *Procès en nullité*, 1:325 and 4:10.

The maid took: Perceval de Cagny, cited in Pernoud and Clin, *Joan of Arc*, 81.

We desire to offer: For the proclamation of ennoblement of Joan and her family, see Quicherat, *Procès de condamnation*, 5:150–53.

She mounted her horse: From Chastellain's *Chroniques*, cited in Pernoud and Clin, *Joan of Arc*, 86.

During that time: Cited in Pernoud and Clin, *Joan of Arc*, 87.

The Maid performed: Pernoud and Clin, *Joan of Arc*, 87.

By the pleasure: Pernoud and Clin, *Joan of Arc*, 90.

Help yourself: Mar. 15, 1431.

On Joan's ransom and the delay of the Duke of Luxembourg, see Nash-Marshall, *Joan of Arc*, 132–35.

On her leap from the tower of Beaurevoir: Trial session of Mar. 3, 1431.

several times in prison ("*plusieurs fois en prison*," etc.): Témoin du Sire Aimon de Macy, May 7, 1456 (in Paris): Duparc, *Procès en nullité*, 4:86.

the English money: "*Achat de monnaie d'or pour solder le prix de la Pucelle*," letters dated Oct. 24 and Dec. 6, 1430: Quicherat, *Procès de condamnation*, 5:190–92.

for service to the king: "*Indemnité à Pierre Cauchon pour les négociations qui précédèrent l'achat de la Pucelle*," letter dated Jan. 31, 1431: Quicherat, *Procès de condamnation*, 5:194–95.

On the different ways in which Joan was assessed by Charles VII and by the English, see the important reflections by Nash-Marshall, *Joan of Arc*, 138–40.

NOTES TO CHAPTER EIGHT: CUNNING AND CLOTHES

They were Englishmen of the lowest sort: Duparc, *Procès en nullité*, 1:431 (my translation). Details of Joan's cell, her shackles and her guards were provided by several witnesses at the nullification trial, most notably Massieu.

Still, some of the men: Duparc, *Procès en nullité*, 1:426.

On the formal course of trial by Inquisition, see Tavard, *Spiritual Way of St. Jeanne d'Arc*, 187.

I see clearly: Duparc, *Procès en nullité*, 1:431.

I was compelled: Duparc, *Procès en nullité*, 1:417–18.

That put me: Duparc, *Procès en nullité*, 1:431.

after seeing: Duparc, *Procès en nullité*, 1:430.

As I saw it then: Duparc, *Procès en nullité*, 1:205.

wanted to get out: Duparc, *Procès en nullité*, 1:228.

Everyone was either: Duparc, *Procès en nullité*, 1:460.

Everything was done: Duparc, *Procès en nullité*, 1:221.

If the English had: Duparc, *Procès en nullité*, 1:240.

We shall ignore him: cited (without attribution) in Scott, *Trial of Joan of Arc*, 11.

When the lord of Beauvais: Duparc, *Procès en nullité*, 1:432.

During the trial: Duparc, *Procès en nullité*, 1:421.

Apparel should be consistent: Aquinas, *Summa Theologica*, II, ii, 169, art. 2, reply to objection 3.

A man should never: Hildegard of Bingen, *Mystical Visions*, book 2, vision 6, 77.

She repeatedly said: Duparc, *Procès en nullité*, 1:181, 426–27.

In her manner: Duparc, *Procès en nullité*, 1:233f.

They convened long hours: Duparc, *Procès en nullité*, 1:448–49.

multum stupefacti: Duparc, *Procès en nullité*, 1:436.

NOTES TO CHAPTER NINE: A DRESS FOR A MASS

God did not say: Colledge and Walsh, *Julian of Norwich*, 165.

NOTES TO CHAPTER TEN: A MATTER OF HONOR

Jean d'Estivet led me: Duparc, *Procès en nullité*, 1:349.

Warwick said that Joan: Duparc, *Procès en nullité*, 1:351.

I just left the room: Duparc, *Procès en nullité*, 1:457.

Jean de Luxembourg wanted: Duparc, *Procès en nullité*, 1:405–6.

For the censures of the University of Paris and the subsequent admonition, see the original Latin texts in Quicherat, *Procès de condamnation*, 1:414–42.

Here are the judges: The abjuration proceedings are preserved in Quicherat, *Procès de condamnation*, 1:442–53.

What she signed: Duparc, *Procès en nullité*, 1:433.

lifelong imprisonment: Quicherat, *Procès de condamnation*, 1:452.

My lord, have no fear: Duparc, *Procès en nullité*, 1:243.

They tore off her dress: Duparc, *Procès en nullité*, 1:209.

I never intended: Duparc, *Procès en nullité*, 1:445.

She received: Duparc, *Procès en nullité*, 1:443.

Joan, go in peace: Jean Massieu (Dec. 17, 1455): Duparc, *Procès en nullité*, 1:435.

She never ceased: Martin Ladvenu (1452): Duparc, *Procès en nullité*, 1:196.

NOTES TO THE AFTERWORD

I was anxious: Duparc, *Procès en nullité*, 1:428.

I wish that my soul: Barrett, *Trial of Jeanne d'Arc*, 436, and Pernoud and Clin, *Joan of Arc*, 207.

We are lost: Duparc, *Procès en nullité*, 1:454.

the just punishment: Barrett, *Trial of Jeanne d'Arc*, 374ff.

Her brief appearance: Duby, *France in the Middle Ages*, 295.

there was no real kingdom: Nash-Marshall, *Joan of Arc*, 165; on nationhood, see 164–72.

Joan taught her people: Nash-Marshall, *Joan of Arc*, 167.

Joan was a being: Churchill, *Heroes of History*, 71.

Bibliography

Late Medieval and Early Renaissance Sources

Actes de la chancellerie d'Henri VI concernant la Normandie sous la domination anglaise (1422–1435). Edited by Paul Casimir Noël Marie Joseph Le Cacheux. 2 vols. Rouen: A. Lestringant, 1907–1908.

d'Auvergne, Martial. "Vigiles du roi Charles VII." In *Poésies* of Martial d'Auvergne. 2 vols. Paris: Urbain Coustelier, 1724.

Basin, Thomas. *Histoire de Charles VII.* Edited and translated by Ch. Samaran. 2 vols. Paris: Les Belles Lettres, 1933 and 1944; revised, 1964.

———. *Histoire de Louis XI.* Edited and translated by Ch. Samaran and M.-C. Gavand. 2 vols. Paris: Les Belles Lettres, 1963, 1966.

Bochon, J. Alexandre. *Choix de chroniques et mémoires sur l'histoire de France avec notes et notices.* Panthéon littéraire, vol. 34 . Paris: A. Desrez, 1838; Delagrave, [n.d.]; Orléans: Herluison, 1875.

Bouvier, Jacques, or Gilles le Bouvier [the so-called Berry Herald]. *Chroniques du roi Charles VII.* Edited by Henri Courteault and Léonce Celier with Marie-Henriette Jullien de Pommerol. Paris: Société de l'Histoire de France/Klincksieck, 1979.

Bueil, Jean de, Count de Sancerre. *Le Jouvencel par Jean de Bueil suivi du commentaire de Guillaume Tringant.* Edited by Camille Favre and Leon Lecestre. 2 vols. Paris: Renouard/H. Laurens, 1887–1889.

Cagny, Perceval de. *Chronique des ducs d'Alençon.* Edited by Henri Moranvillé. Paris: Société de l'Histoire de France/Klincksieck, 1902; 1982.

Chartier, Alain. *Epistola de puella.* In *Oeuvres latines.* Edited by Pascale Bourgain-Hemeryck. Paris: Sources d'Histoire Medievale/IRHT/CNRS, 1977.

Chartier, Jean. *Chronique de Charles VII.* Edited by Auguste Vallet de Viriville. 3 vols. Paris: P, Jannet, 1858.

——. "La chronique latine de Jean Chartier (1422–1450)." Edited by Charles Samaran. *Annuaire-Bulletin de la Société de l'Histoire de France* (1926), 183–273.

Chastellain, Georges. *Chronique des ducs de Bourgogne.* Edited by Kervyn de Lettenhove, in his edition of the Oeuvres of Chastellain. 5 vols. Brussels: Académie Royale de Belgique, 1863–1866.

Chronique de la Pucelle ou chronique de Cousinot, suivie de la chronique Normand de P. Cochon, relatives aux régnes de Charles VI et de Charles VII, restituées à leurs auteurs et publiées pour la première fois intégralement à partir de Van 1403, d'après les manuscrits, avec notices, notes, et développements. Edited by Auguste Vallet de Viriville. Paris: Bibliothèque gauloise/Adolphe Delahaye, 1859; reprint, Gamier, 1888.

Chronique de Mont-Saint-Michel (1343–1468). Edited by Siméon Luce. 2 vols. Paris: Société des Anciens Textes Français/Firmin Didot, 1879–1883.

Macon, Jean de. *Chronique du siège d'Orléans et de l'établissement de la fete du 8 mai 1429.* Edited by Boucher de Molandon. In *Mémoires de la Société historique de l'Orléanais* 18 (1884): 241–348. Orléans: Herluison, 1883; also edited by André Salmon in Bibliothèque de L'École des Chartres 8 (1847): 500–509. An anonymous chronicle found in the Vatican and in St. Petersburg. Also: *Chronique Martiniane: Edi-*

tion critique d'une interpolation pour le règne de Charles VII restituée à Jean Le Clerc. Edited by Pierre Champion. Paris: Bibliothèque du XVe siècle/Honoré Champion, 1907. *Chroniques de France/Chronique de Saint-Denis, depuis les Troiens jusqu'à la mort de Charles VII en 1461.* J. Viard, ed. Société de l'Histoire de France. 3 vols. Paris: Renouard, 1920–1953.

Cochon, Pierre [not Pierre Cauchon, bishop of Beauvais]. *Chronique normande.* Edited by Ch. de Robillard de Beaurepaire. Rouen: Le Brument, 1870.

Doncoeur, Paul, SJ, ed. *La Minute Française des Intérrogatoires de Jeanne la Pucelle, d'après le Réquisitoire de Jean d'Estivet et les manuscrits de d'Urfé et d'Orléans.* Melun: Librairie D'Argences, 1952.

Gerson, Jean [le Charlier de]. *De mirabili Victoria.* In *Opera,* edited by Ellies Dupin. Vol. 4. Antwerp/The Hague, 1706.

————. *De quadam puella.* English translation in "Jean Gerson's Theological Treatise and Other Memoirs in Defence of Joan of Arc." *Revue de l'Université d'Ottawa* 41 (1971): 58–80. Also in Quicherat and in J. B. Monnayeur, *Traité de Jean Gerson sur la Pucelle.* Paris: Champion, 1910.

Giraut, Guillaume. "Note de Guillaume Giraut sur la levée du siège d'Orléans." Edited by Boucher de Molandon. *Mémoires de la Société Archéologique de l'Orléanais* 4 (1858).

Gruel, Guillaume [the Younger]. *Chronique d'Arthur de Richemont.* Edited by Achille Levavasseur. Paris: Société de l'Histoire de France/Renouard, 1890. See also: Fauquembergue, Clément de. *Journal de Clément de Fauquembergue.* Edited by Alexandre Tuetey and Henri Lacaille. (1903–1915) Paris: Société de l'Histoire de France/Renouard, 3 vols. *Journal d'un Bourgeois de Paris, 1405–1449.* Alexandre Tuetey, ed. Société de l'Histoire de France (Paris: Renouard, 1881). *Journal d'un Bourgeois de Paris, sous Charles VI et Charles VII.* André Mary, ed. Paris: Jonquières, 1929. *Journal du siège d'Orléans et du Voyage de Reims, 1428–29, augmenté de plusieurs documents, notamment des Comptes de ville*. P. Charpentier and Ch. Cuissard, eds. Orléans: Cuissard, 1896.

Le Fèvre de Saint-Rémy, Jean. *Chronique*. Edited by F. Morand. Société de l'Histoire de France, 2 vols. Paris: Renouard, 1876–1881.

Monk of Saint-Rémy/Michael Pintoin (1349?–1421). *Chronicorum Karoli Sexti/Chronique du religieux de Saint-Denys, contenant le régne de Charles VI de 1380 à 1422/Chronique de Charles VI. See Louis-François Bellaguet*. 6 vols. Paris: Impr. de Crapelet, 1839–1852; 6 vols. in 3, edited and translated, with introduction, by Bernard Guenée. Paris: Editions du Comité des travaux historiques et scientifiques, 1994.

Monstrelet, Enguerrand de. *Chronique: 1400–1444*. Edited by L. Douët d'Arcq. 6 vols. Paris: Société de l'Histoire de France/Renouard, 1857–1862. Also: *Le Mistére du siège d'Orléans, publié pour la première fois, d'après le manuscrit unique conservé à la Bibliothèque du Vatican*. Edited by François Guessard and Eugène de Certain. Documents inédits sur l'histoire de France. Paris: Imprimerie impériale, 1862.

Morisini, Antonio. *Chronique: Extraits rélatifs à l'histoire de France*. Edited and translated by L. Dorez, with introduction and notes by Germain Lefèvre-Pontalis. Paris: Société de l'Histoire de France/Renouard, 1898–1902.

Nangis, Guillaume de. *Chronique parisienne anonyme de 1316 à 1339, précédée d'additions à la Chronique française dite de Guillaume de Nangis*. Edited by A. Hellot. *Mémoires de la Société de l'Histoire de Paris et de l'Ile-de-France* 2 (1884): 1–207.

Wavrin [du Forestel], Jean de. *Anchiennes chroniques d'engleterre*. Edited by Emilie Dupont. 3 vols. Paris: Société de l'Histoire/Renouard, 1858–1863.

———. *Recueil de chroniques et anchiennes istoires de la Grant Bretaigne a present nommee Engleterre*. Edited and translated by William Hardy. Rolls Series 39. 5 vols. (1–2 in English trans.) London: Her Majesty's Stationer's Office, 1891.

von Windecken, Eberhard. *Denkwürdigkeiten zur Geschichte des Zeitalters Kaiser Sigmunds.* In *Les sources allemandes de l'histoire de Jeanne d'Arc,* edited and translated by Germain Lefèvre-Pontalis. Paris: Société de l'Histoire de France/Renouard, 1903.

Additional Sources

Armstrong, Regis J., OFM Cap.; J. A. Wayne Hellmann, OFM Conv.; and William J. Short, OFM, eds. *Francis of Assisi: Early Documents.* 3 vols. New York: New City Press, 1999–2001.

Barrett, W. P., trans. *The Trial of Jeanne d'Arc,* with additional material by Pierre Champion. Translated by Coley Taylor and Ruth H. Kerr. London: Routledge, 1931; New York: Gotham House, 1932.

Boccaccio, Giovanni. *The Decameron.* Translated by J. M. Rigg. Vol. 1. London: Navarre Society, 1921.

Bouteiller, E. de, and G. de Braux. *Nouvelles récherches sur la famille de Jeanne d'Arc. Enquêtes inédites.* Paris et Orléans: Généaologie, 1879.

Bouvier, Gilles le. *Chroniques du roi Charles VII.* Edited by Henri Courteault, Léonce Celier, and Marie-Henriette Jullien de Pommerol. Paris: Klincksieck/Société de l'Histoire de France, 1979.

Brooks, Polly Schoyer. *Beyond the Myth: The Story of Joan of Arc.* Boston: Houghton Mifflin, 1990.

Champion, Pierre. *Le Procès de condemnation de Jeanne d'Arc.* 2 vols. Paris: Edouard Champion, 1920–1921.

Churchill, Winston. *Heroes of History.* London: Cassell, 1968; New York: Dodd, Mead & Co., 1968.

Colledge, Edmund, OSA, and James Walsh, SJ, trans. *Julian of Norwich: Showings.* New York: Paulist Press, 1978.

Colrat, Jean-Claude. *Compagnons d'armes de Jeanne La Pucelle.* 3 vols. Orléans: Le Briquet, 1992.

DeVries, Kelly. "A Woman as Leader of Men: Joan of Arc's Military Career." In *Fresh Verdicts on Joan of Arc,* edited by Bonnie Wheeler and Charles T. Wood, 3–18. New York and London: Garland Publishing, 1996.

Doncoeur, Paul, and Yvonne Lanhers, eds. *Documents et Récherches Rélatifs à Jeanne La Pucelle: La Réhabilitation Épiscopale du Procès de 1455–1456.* Paris: Desclée de Brouwer, 1961.

Duby, Georges. *France in the Middle Ages, 987–1460: From Hugh Capet to Joan of Arc.* Translated by Juliet Vale. Oxford and Cambridge: Blackwell, 1991.

Duparc, Pierre, ed. *Procès en nullité de la condemnation de Jeanne d'Arc.* 5 vols. Paris: Société de l'Histoire de France/Klincksieck, 1977–1989.

Fatula, Mary Ann. *Catherine of Siena's Way.* London: Darton, Longman & Todd, 1987.

Fowler, Kenneth A., ed. *The Hundred Years War.* New York and London: Macmillan, 1971.

Fraioli, Deborah A. *Joan of Arc: The Early Debate.* Rochester, NY: Boydell & Brewer, 2000.

Gies, Frances. *Joan of Arc: The Legend and the Reality.* New York: Harper & Row, 1981.

Gower, Ronald Sutherland. *Joan of Arc.* London: John C. Nimmo, 1893.

Hildegard von Bingen. *Mystical Visions.* Translated by Bruce Hozeski. Santa Fe: Bear & Co., 1995.

Hughson, Thomas D., SJ. "Joan, L'Agent Provocateur." In *Joan of Arc at the University,* edited by Mary Elizabeth Tallon, 59 ff. Milwaukee: Marquette University Press, 1997.

Kennedy, Angus J., and Kenneth Varty, eds. *Ditié de Jehanne d'Arc de Christine de Pisan.* Medium Aevum Monographs, new series 9. Oxford: Society for the Study of Medieval Languages and Literature, 1977.

Lewis, C. S. *Letters to Malcolm: Chiefly on Prayer.* Glasgow: Collins/
Fontana, 1977.

Marcantel, Pamela. *An Army of Angels: A Novel of Joan of Arc.* New York:
St. Martin's Griffin, 1997.

McBrien, Richard P. *Lives of the Popes.* San Francisco: HarperSanFrancisco, 1997.

Monstrelet, Enguerrand de. *The Chronicles.* London: William Smith,
1840; George Routledge, 1867.

Morel, H. "La noblesse de la famille de Jeanne d'Arc au XVIe siècle."
Société d'histoire du droit—Collection d'histoire institutionnelle et sociale
4 (1972).

Murray, T. Douglas. *Joan of Arc, Maid of Orléans and Deliverer of France.*
London: Heinemann, 1902.

Nash-Marshall, Siobhan. *Joan of Arc: A Spiritual Biography.* New York:
Crossroad, 1999.

———. "On the Fate of Nations." *Logos: A Journal of Catholic Thought
and Culture* 4, no. 2 (Spring 2001): 32–65.

Nicolle, David. *Orléans 1429: France Turns the Tide.* Botley, Oxford:
Osprey Publishing, 2001.

Pernoud, Régine. *Joan of Arc, By Herself and Her Witnesses.* Translated
by Edward Hyams. New York: Stein and Day, 1966. First published
in French as *Jeanne d'Arc par elle-même et par ses témoins*, 1962.

———. *The Retrial of Joan of Arc: The Evidence at the Trial for Her Reha-
bilitation.* Translated by J. M. Cohen. London: Methuen, 1955.

Pernoud, Régine, and Marie-Véronique Clin. *Joan of Arc: Her Story.*
Translated and revised by Jeremy duQuesnay Adams. New York: St.
Martin's Griffin, 1998.

Perroy, Edouard. *The Hundred Years War.* Translated by W. ᴾ
London: Eyre & Spottiswoode, 1951.

Quicherat, Jules-Étienne-Joseph, ed. *Procès de condam*
itation de Jeanne d'Arc, dite la Pucelle: Publiés pou
d'après les manuscrits de la Bibliothèque Nationale, s

documents historiques qu'on a pu réunir et accompagnés de notes et déclaircissements. 5 vols. Sociéte de l'Histoire de France. Paris: Jules Renouard, 1841–1849.

Scott, W. S., trans. *The Trial of Joan of Arc: Being the Verbatim Report of the Proceedings from the Orléans Manuscript.* London: Folio Society, 1956.

Shaw, Bernard. *Saint Joan: A Chronicle Play in Six Scenes and an Epilogue (1924).* Baltimore: Penguin Books, 1951.

Tallon, Mary Elizabeth, ed. *Joan of Arc at the University.* Milwaukee: Marquette University Press, 1997.

Tavard, George H. *The Spiritual Way of St. Jeanne d'Arc.* Collegeville, MN: Liturgical Press/Michael Glazier, 1998.

Tisset, Pierre, and Yvonne Lanhers, eds. and trans. *Procès de condamnation de Jeanne d'Arc.* 3 vols. Société de l'Histoire de France. Paris: Klincksieck, 1960, 1970, 1971.

Wheeler, Bonnie, and Charles T. Wood, eds. *Fresh Verdicts on Joan of Arc.* New York and London: Garland Publishing, 1996.

Willard, Charity Cannon. *Christine de Pizan: Her Life and Works.* New York: Persea Books, 1984.

Wood, Charles T. "Joan of Arc's Mission and the Lost Record of Her Interrogation at Poitiers." In *Fresh Verdicts on Joan of Arc,* edited by Bonnie Wheeler and Charles T. Wood, 19–30. New York and London: Garland Publishing, 1996.